Easy Access
for Windows 95

Jeffry Byrne

Easy Access for Windows 95

Copyright © 1995 by Que® Corporation.

Library of Congress Catalog Card Number: 95-71417

International Standard Book Number: 0-29236-0607-5

98 97 96 95   8 7 6 5 4 3 2 1

Interpretation of the printing code: the rightmost double-digit number is the year of the book's first printing; the rightmost single-digit number is the number of the book's printing. For example, a printing code of 95-1 shows that this copy of the book was printed during the first printing of the book in 1995.

Screen reproductions in this book were created by means of the program Collage Plus from Inner Media, Inc., Hollis, NH.

Dedication

To my wife, Marisa. Thanks for all the years of support, help, and encouragement.

Credits

Publisher
Roland Elgey

Vice President and Publisher
Marie Butler-Knight

Publishing Manager
Barry Pruett

Editorial Services Director
Elizabeth Keaffaber

Managing Editor
Michael Cunningham

Product Development Specialist
David Bradford

Production Editor
Phil Kitchel

Copy Editor
Rebecca Mayfield

Technical Editor
C. Herbert Feltner

Book Designers
Barbara Kordesh
Amy Peppler-Adams

Cover Designers
Dan Armstrong
Kim Scott

Production Team
Claudia Bell
Anne Dickerson
Michael Thomas
Scott Tullis
Kelly Warner

Indexer
Gina Brown

Composed in *Stone Serif* and *MCPdigital* by Que Corporation

About the Author

Jeffry Byrne has been working with and teaching others about computers for over fifteen years. He is the author of numerous computer books in three languages, including titles on Microsoft Access, Borland's Quattro Pro and Paradox for Windows and DOS, Intuit's Quickbooks for Windows, and Computer Associate's CA-Simply Money. He has been on the beta test teams for most of these products and for other accounting and database software. When not writing and testing software, Jeff works as the purchasing manager for a Portland, Oregon-based network VAR and computer retailer. You can contact Jeff through CompuServe (71553,1660).

Acknowledgments

I would like to thank Martha O'Sullivan for allowing me to create this book, and David Bradford for his help in ensuring that everything went the way it should. Special thanks are due to Phil Kitchel for keeping to the tight production schedule and to Rebecca Mayfield for her excellent editing. Also to all of the other people at Que who have had a hand in this project.

Contents

Part III: Entering and Editing Data 77

Part IV: Using Database Forms 117

Part V: Getting Information from a Database — 165

Part VI: Creating and Using Reports — 191

Part VII: Combining Information — 215

Part VIII: Reference — 229

Index — 236

Introduction

This book is designed with you, the beginner, in mind. The tasks in this book are designed to help you get up and running by guiding you through many common database operations.

What You Can Do with Access

Every day you work with many databases: your personal phone directory, a customer list, a product catalog, employee records, or information in a filing cabinet. With Microsoft Access for Windows 95 you can build a database that can store and manipulate any information that you need to use. You can use Microsoft Access for Windows 95 to carry out these specific tasks:

- *Create a personal address and phone list.* Keep your own address and phone list up-to-date. By using a Microsoft Access for Windows 95 table to maintain your address book, you never have to cross out old addresses and phone numbers again, or have to recopy all of the entries into a new book.

- *Maintain mailing lists and labels.* With Microsoft Access for Windows 95, you can easily create and maintain small or large mailing lists. If a friend or customer moves, simply changing their address in a single table takes only a few seconds. You can print labels in a snap by using the report function.

- *Keep a list of customer contacts.* If you are a salesperson, you can use Microsoft Access for Windows 95 to keep track of sales calls to your customers. By keeping closer tabs of individual details about each customer, you can more easily meet needs of customers—and increase sales at the same time.

- *Build sales reports.* You can use Microsoft Access for Windows 95 to build a complete reporting system to view your sales by time period, by salesperson, or by product. You can now see up-to-date information about the performance of a specific item, or the accomplishments of a specific salesperson. You can print or display reports.

- *Create a sales order database.* You can use Microsoft Access for Windows 95 to build a complete data-entry system to track your sales, customers, and shipment of products. The sample database NWIND, provided with Access, shows a good example of such a system.

- *Build an inventory control system.* Controlling the flow of products that are bought and sold is probably one of the most difficult jobs for a business. By tying an inventory-control system to your sales order system, you can quickly get a firm grasp of the ebb and flow of your own inventory, and your cash.

Easy Access for Windows 95 is divided into eight parts. Each part is concerned with a different aspect of Access, and each successive part is built on information that you learn from earlier parts:

■ *Microsoft Access for Windows 95 is easy to use, but it's still a complex beast.* Part I, "Learning the Basics," provides an introduction to the most common features and tasks.

■ *You can store any type of information in a Microsoft Access for Windows 95 table.* You can easily build a table to store any information that you want to track. You can use tables to store data about employees, inventory, orders, stamps, coins, or your plants in your yard. In Part II of this book, "Using a Database," you learn to construct a table to store various types of information.

■ *You can quickly and easily change information in the database.* If a supplier's phone number or address changes, you simply have to change this information in the supplier's table. Access changes the new address and phone number on your purchase orders and accounts payable forms and reports. These tasks are covered in Part III, "Entering and Editing Data."

■ *You can create a form to display information in a familiar way.* By using forms to show the information from a table, you can easily view an entire record in a familiar format. If you have a paper form that you now use, you can easily design an Access form that looks and works like the form you already use. These tasks are covered in Part IV, "Using Database Forms."

■ *You can choose selected records from your database that meet criteria that you specify.* For example, instead of searching through all your customer files to find who bought green widgets last month, you can query Microsoft Access for Windows 95 to find and display this information. Tasks that show you how to build a query are included in Part V, "Getting Information from a Database."

■ *You can create printed reports from the information contained in your database.* For example, you can print a report that displays a summary of your sales over the last month and group the information by salesperson or by item sold. These tasks are covered in Part VI, "Creating and Using Reports."

■ *You can create even more powerful forms and reports by combining information from more than one table.* By using a query to select specific data from two or more tables, you can view, add, or edit information in each of the tables. Forms and reports can use a query to select and display related information from several sources. These tasks are covered in Part VII, "Combining Information."

■ Part VIII is a listing of the most commonly used commands and functions and their keyboard equivalents. The icon buttons on the various toolbars and toolboxes that you will use are also displayed, along with a short description of each.

Task Sections

Big Screen

At the beginning of each task is a large screen shot that shows how the computer screen looks after you complete the procedure that follows in that task. Sometimes the screen shot shows a feature discussed in that task, such as a shortcut menu.

TASK 1

Starting Access from the Start Button

"Why would I do this?"

Access is a database program that operates only within the Windows 95 environment. Once you install Access on your computer system, you can start the program with the Start button on the taskbar at the bottom of your screen. You use the Start button to locate a file or start a program.

Step-by-Step Screens

Each task includes a screen shot for each step
of the procedure. The screen shot shows how
your computer screen looks at each point
along the way.

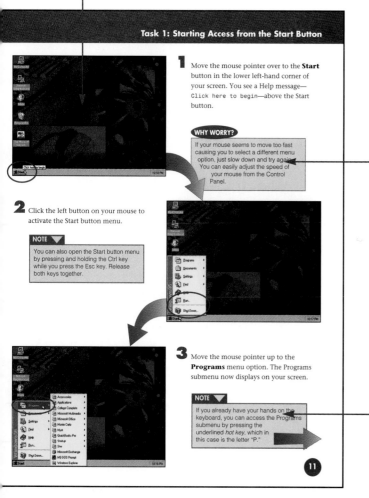

Task 1: Starting Access from the Start Button

1 Move the mouse pointer over to the **Start**
button in the lower left-hand corner of
your screen. You see a Help message—
Click here to begin—above the Start
button.

WHY WORRY?

If your mouse seems to move too fast
causing you to select a different menu
option, just slow down and try again.
You can easily adjust the speed of
your mouse from the Control
Panel.

2 Click the left button on your mouse to
activate the Start button menu.

NOTE

You can also open the Start button menu
by pressing and holding the Ctrl key
while you press the Esc key. Release
both keys together.

3 Move the mouse pointer up to the
Programs menu option. The Programs
submenu now displays on your screen.

NOTE

If you already have your hands on the
keyboard, you can access the Programs
submenu by pressing the
underlined *hot key,* which in
this case is the letter "P."

Why Worry? Notes

You may find that you performed a task, such
as opening a table, that you didn't want to do
after all. These notes tell you how to undo
certain procedures or get out of a situation,
such as displaying a Help screen or moving
ahead anyway.

Notes

Many tasks include short notes that tell you
a little more about certain procedures. These
notes define terms, explain other options,
refer you to other sections when applicable,
and so on.

11

5

PART I

Learning the Basics

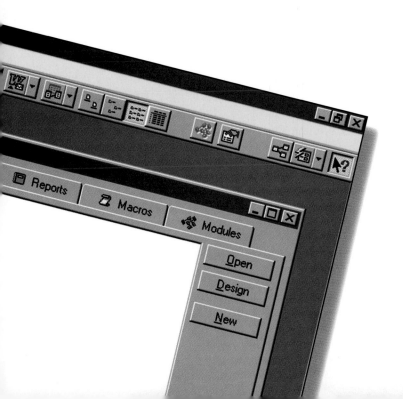

Part I introduces you to Microsoft Access for Windows 95—referred to as *Access* throughout the rest of this book—and shows you how to start the program and use the menu bar and toolbars. This book is designed with you, the beginner, in mind. This part of *Easy Access* also acquaints you with the Access Help system and shows you how to exit or close the program. The tasks in this book help you get up and running with Access by guiding you through many common database operations. You learn the simplest way to perform each operation, usually using a mouse. Specifically, in this part you learn:

■ What an Access database is

■ How to use a mouse with Access for Windows 95

■ How to use the Access Desktop window

■ How to open an existing database file

■ How to select a menu command

■ How to use the mouse to select a toolbar button or tab button

■ How to use Help and the Answer Wizard

■ How to start and exit Access

■ How to create a shortcut for Access to place on your desktop

Before you continue with *Easy Access* you should be familiar with a few simple database concepts and terms. A database consists of one or more *tables*. A table contains *rows* and *columns*.

Each row of a table is a *record*. The record consists of all of the information about a single entry in the table. One record may contain a customer's name, address, telephone number, credit limit, and customer number. Another table may contain records about products: product ID, name, cost, selling price, quantity on hand, quantity on order, and supplier ID.

Each column of the table is a *field*. A field is the smallest distinct pieceof information a record contains. You may have individual fields for a customer's last name, first name, street address, city, state, ZIP code, and customer ID number.

Generally, several tables that are related to each other in some way make up a database. Each table holds a specific part of the database. One table may contain information about customers; another table holds information about orders; and a third table has information about the products that you sell. You use queries, forms, and reports to combine and join information from the table.

In this part of *Easy Access*, you learn how to open an Access database file, select menu commands, and use the Toolbar. This part also covers the Help system. If you already have experience using Windows 95 (you know how to open and exit programs and use Windows 95 style menus), you may want to skip to Task 4. If Windows 95 is new to you, be sure to take a few minutes to read through this part and try each of the tasks before you continue.

Although you access most Access features using either the mouse or keyboard, many functions are much easier when you use the mouse. However, you can input information into a field only with a keyboard.

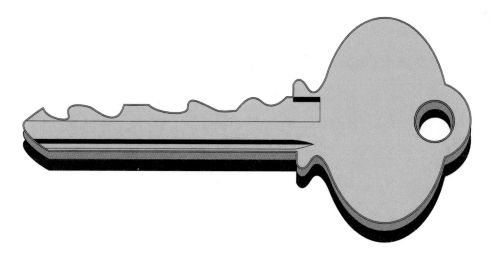

Starting Access from the Start Button

"Why would I do this?"

Access is a database program that operates only within the Windows 95 environment. Once you install Access on your computer system, you can start the program with the Start button on the taskbar at the bottom of your screen. You use the Start button to locate a file or start a program.

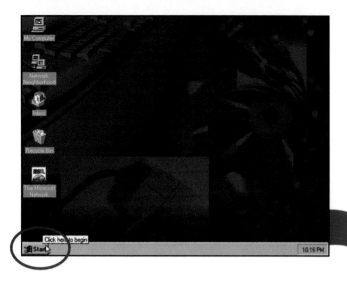

1 Move the mouse pointer over to the **Start** button in the lower left-hand corner of your screen. You see a Help message— Click here to begin—above the Start button.

WHY WORRY?

If your mouse seems to move too fast causing you to select a different menu option, just slow down and try again. You can easily adjust the speed of your mouse from the Control Panel.

2 Click the left button on your mouse to activate the Start button menu.

NOTE ▼

You can also open the Start button menu by pressing and holding the Ctrl key while you press the Esc key. Release both keys together.

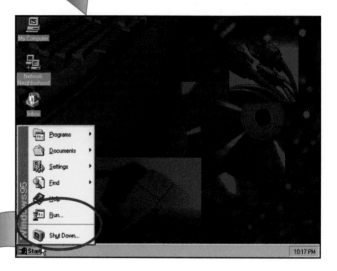

3 Move the mouse pointer up to the **Programs** menu option. The Programs submenu now displays on your screen.

NOTE ▼

If you already have your hands on the keyboard, you can access the Programs submenu by pressing the underlined *hot key*, which in this case is the letter "P."

4 Choose the **Microsoft Access** option from the menu, and your computer loads Access into memory so that you can use it. ■

WHY WORRY?

If Access does not start, simply try again. Perhaps you selected the wrong menu item inadvertently.

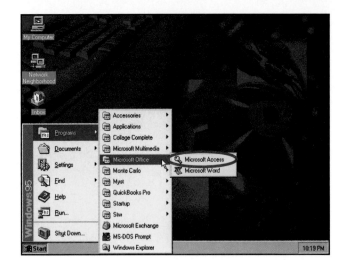

Opening an Existing Database

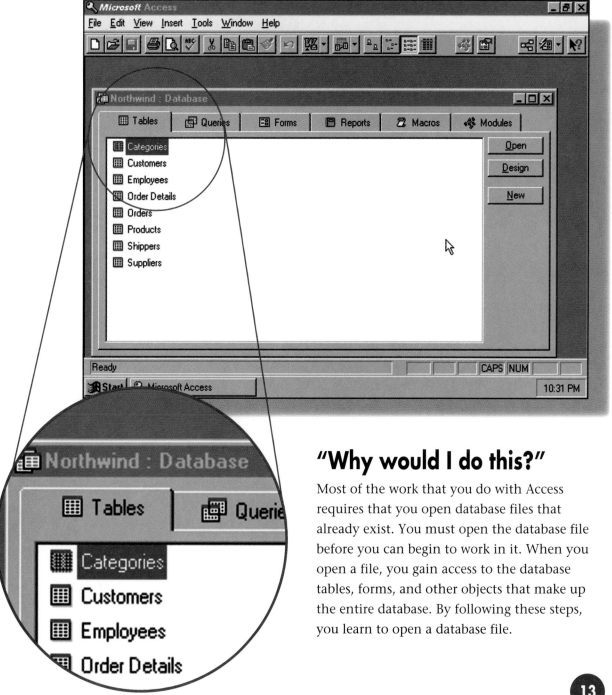

"Why would I do this?"

Most of the work that you do with Access requires that you open database files that already exist. You must open the database file before you can begin to work in it. When you open a file, you gain access to the database tables, forms, and other objects that make up the entire database. By following these steps, you learn to open a database file.

1 You see this dialog box when you load Access. Be sure to select the **Open an Existing Database** option button. A black dot in the option button means that it is selected. If one of the other options is selected, click your option once to select it.

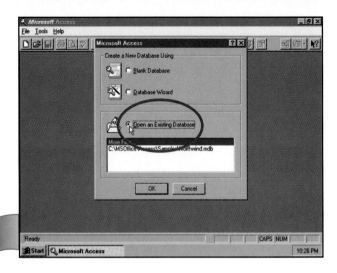

2 Move the mouse pointer to the filename `C:\MSOffice\Access\Samples\Northwind.mdb` and click to select it. This is the sample database file that Microsoft provides with your Access program.

NOTE ▼

If you do not see the Northwind database filename, click the More Files option to see if it is in another location. If you still can't find it, you may need to rerun the Access Setup program and install the sample files.

3 Click the **OK** button at the bottom of the dialog box, and then click the **OK** button on the Northwind Traders opening screen. ∎

WHY WORRY?

If you open a different database file simply click the Close button at the upper-right corner of your screen. You can then try steps 1 through 3 again.

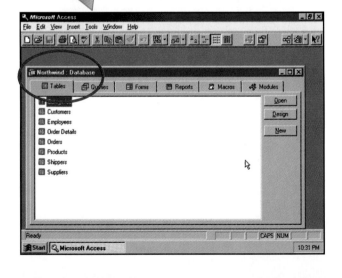

Using Menu Commands

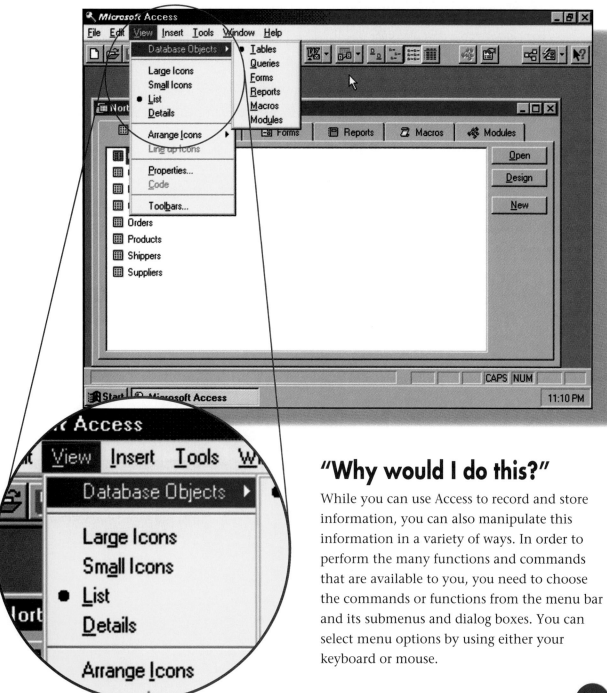

"Why would I do this?"

While you can use Access to record and store information, you can also manipulate this information in a variety of ways. In order to perform the many functions and commands that are available to you, you need to choose the commands or functions from the menu bar and its submenus and dialog boxes. You can select menu options by using either your keyboard or mouse.

1 Move the mouse pointer to the **File** menu option and click the left mouse button once. This opens the drop-down File menu.

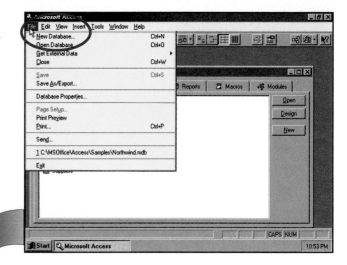

NOTE

You see some menu options have a two-key combination to the right. You can access these menu options without going through the menus by pressing the Ctrl key and the indicated letter.

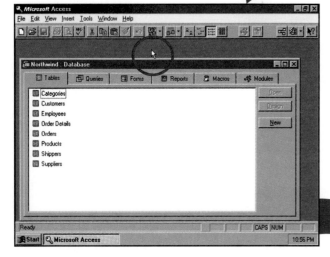

2 Move the mouse away from the menu bar and the drop-down menu; click once to deselect both.

3 Press the **Alt** key on your keyboard to access the menu bar and then press the **V** key. You see the View menu drop down on-screen. An underlined letter in a menu command or option is the hot key. You can use the hot key by pressing the underlined letter on the keyboard.

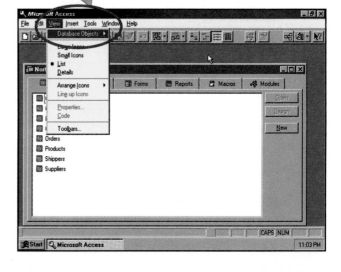

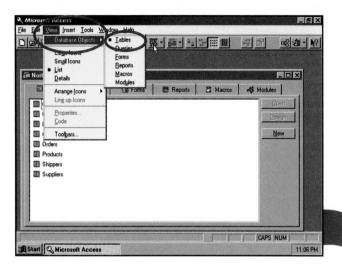

4 Choose the **Database Objects** option from the menu. You see a submenu appear that lists the six Access object groups. The current object group is indicated by the bullet beside the menu option.

5 Select **Forms** from the submenu. You see the Database window change from the Tables group to the Forms group. ■

WHY WORRY?

If you decide that you do not want to switch to a different Access object group, just press the Esc key and back out of the menu. Each time you press the Esc key, you move back to the previous menu option.

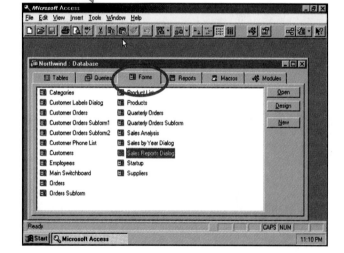

17

Using Toolbar Buttons and Tabs

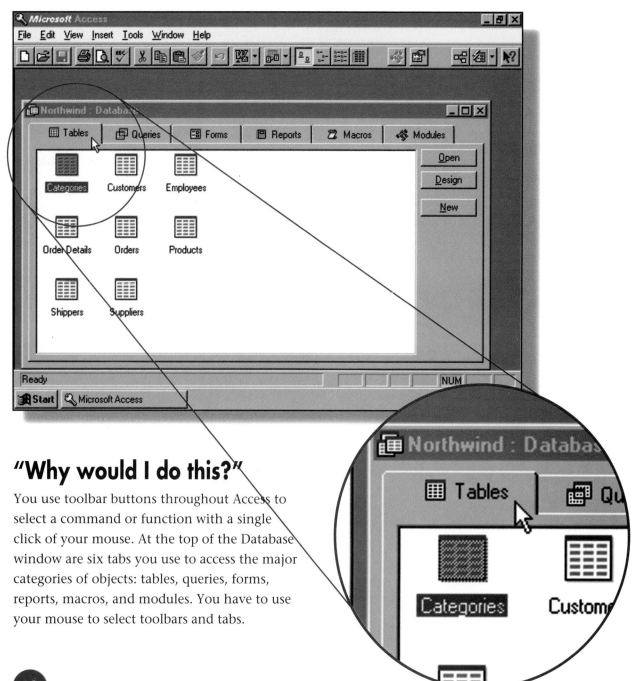

"Why would I do this?"

You use toolbar buttons throughout Access to select a command or function with a single click of your mouse. At the top of the Database window are six tabs you use to access the major categories of objects: tables, queries, forms, reports, macros, and modules. You have to use your mouse to select toolbars and tabs.

1 To use a toolbar button, place the mouse pointer on it. In this example, position the mouse pointer over the **Large Icons** button.

NOTE

You see a description of the button—called a ToolTip—appear beneath it when you pause the mouse pointer on top of the button. You can turn ToolTips on or off in the Toolbars dialog box. (Select View, Toolbars to open this dialog box.)

2 Click the left mouse button once to activate the function for the selected toolbar button. You see the form's options listed in the Database window change to large icons. You select all toolbar buttons this way.

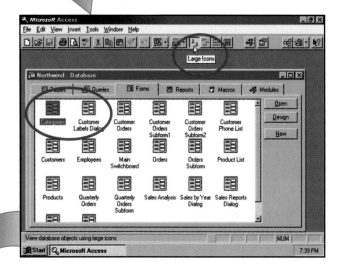

3 You use tabs to access the six primary groups of objects that compose Access. When you open the program, the Tables tab is the default tab. Move the mouse pointer to the **Tables** tab.

4 Click the Table tab once. You see the list of tables appear in the Database window once again.

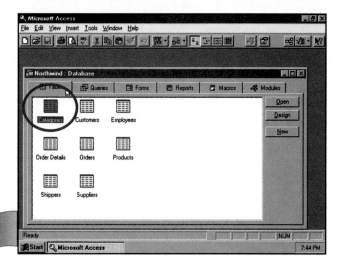

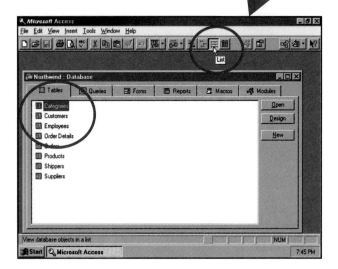

5 Move the mouse pointer to the **List** button and click once to revert the Database window lists to the default format. ■

WHY WORRY?

Just reselect a tab if you select one other than the one that you need. Selecting a tab simply displays the list of objects that are available to you.

Getting Help

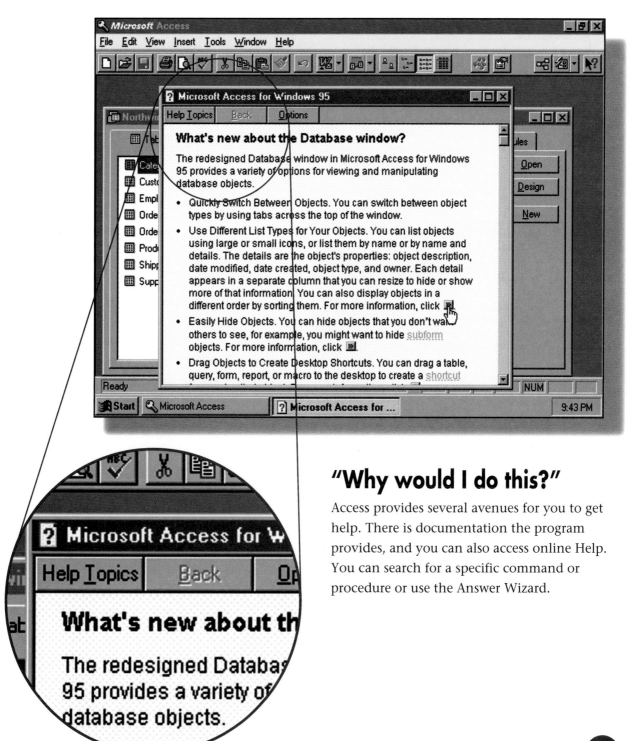

"Why would I do this?"

Access provides several avenues for you to get help. There is documentation the program provides, and you can also access online Help. You can search for a specific command or procedure or use the Answer Wizard.

21

1 Click **Help** on the menu bar. This displays the Help menu with the available list of help options.

NOTE ▼

You can click on each of the Contents tab's books to view additional subtopics and details about a particular subject. Double-clicking the book icon again closes it and the subtopics.

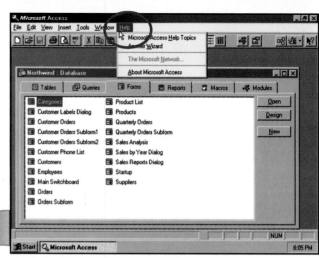

2 Select the first option on the menu, **Microsoft Access Help Topics**. After a moment, you see the Help Topics dialog box appear on your screen. This screen has four tabs: Contents, Index, Find, and Answer Wizard. You can use any of these tabs to access different kinds of help. Here you see the list from the Contents tab.

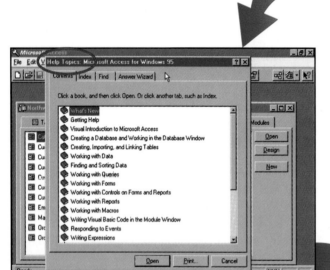

3 Double-click on the book icon **What's New**. You see the book icon change from a closed book to an open book as subtopics appear beneath the main topic. Some topics have many subtopics.

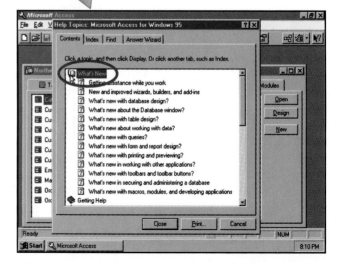

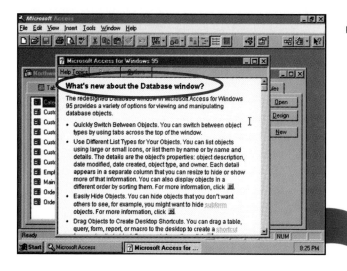

4 Double-click the question mark icon for the subtopic `What's new about the Database window?` to view information about this topic. The screen that appears displays information about the selected topic and enables you to choose new selections of subtopics if additional subtopics are available.

5 Move the mouse pointer to the word `shortcut` (it appears in green and is underlined) this is called *jump text*. You see the mouse pointer change shape; it now resembles a hand with a pointing index finger. Position the tip of the index finger on the button and click. Click again to remove the definition.

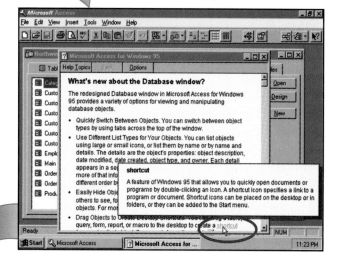

6 Move the mouse pointer to the first button labeled `For more information, click`. When the pointer again changes to a pointing hand, click the button to view a new help screen.

7 Click the **Help Topics** button to return to the Help Topics dialog box. Choose the next tab, **Index**. You now see the Index dialog box. When you type the key words of your help subject in the text box, Access displays the topics in the list box below that most closely match what you type.

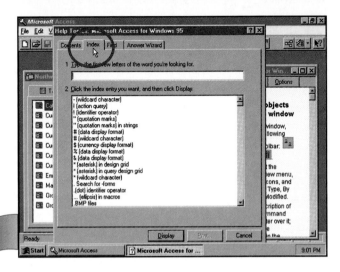

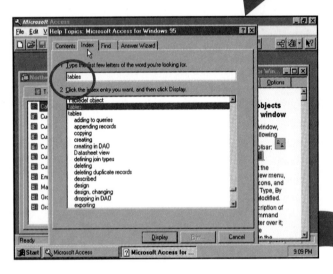

8 Type what you want to find in the Index tab's text box. Watch the list box below move through the listings as you type. Once you see an index option that you want more information on, click on it to select it. You see your entry in the text box change to match the index entry.

9 To view the specific help message for an entry, select **tables, creating** and click the **Display** button. You see a new Topics Found dialog box.

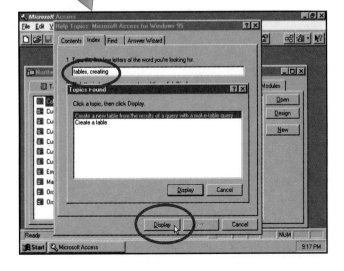

NOTE ▼

The Access Help system has two very similar features: Index and Find. This task covers the simpler of the two, Index. Find is a more extensive version of Index; you can access Find by clicking the Find tab. This opens the Find dialog box. Try it.

24

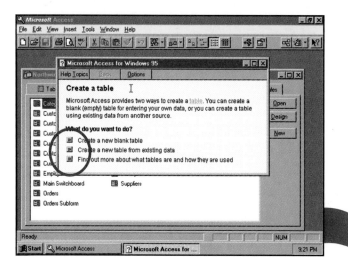

10 Select the second topic and click the **Display** button. You now see the next help dialog box. This dialog box gives you several new options that you can select by clicking the buttons beside the choices listed under What do you want to do?

11 Click the **Help Topics** button to return to the Help Topics dialog box. Select the **Answer Wizard** tab. With the Answer Wizard you can type a short sentence about what you need help on. Type **create a new table**.

> **NOTE** ▼
>
> The Answer Wizard is also available to you directly from the Help menu.

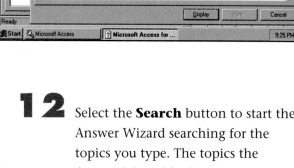

12 Select the **Search** button to start the Answer Wizard searching for the topics you type. The topics the Answer Wizard finds appear in the list box in the lower half of the tab.

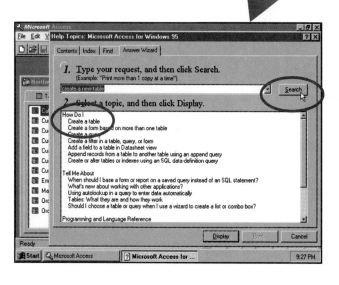

13

Select the topic **How Do I Create a table** and click the **Display** button to view more information. Move the mouse pointer to the first option, **Create a new blank table**.

NOTE ▼

Remember, you can also double-click the selected topic to immediately jump to its information screen.

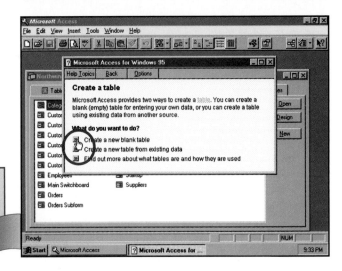

14

Click the button to see information about creating a new blank table. Notice that there are many words that appear as jump text; when you click one of these words, Access displays a short definition for the term.

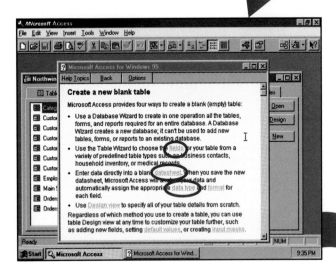

15

To return to the Access program window, click on the **Close** button in the Help Topics dialog box. ■

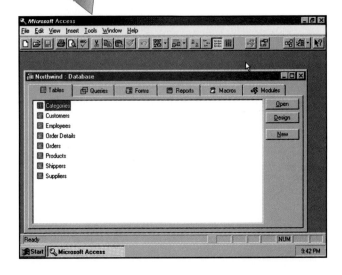

Using Context-Sensitive Help

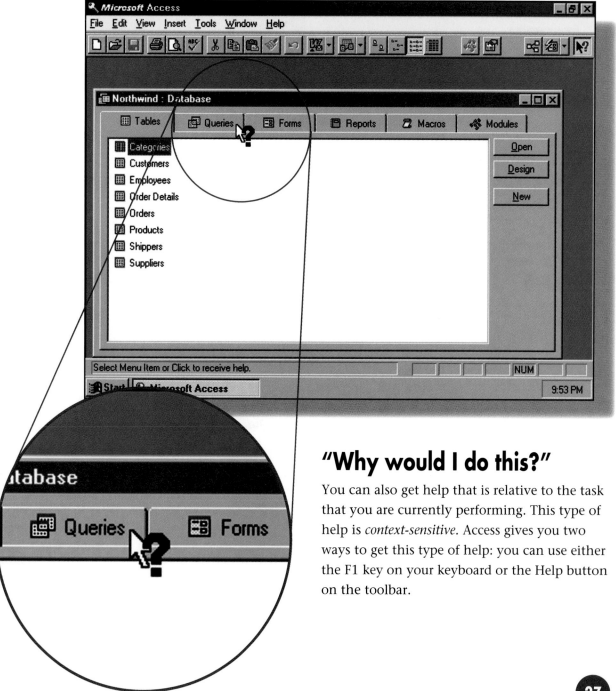

"Why would I do this?"

You can also get help that is relative to the task that you are currently performing. This type of help is *context-sensitive*. Access gives you two ways to get this type of help: you can use either the F1 key on your keyboard or the Help button on the toolbar.

1 Click the **Help** button located at the right end of the toolbar. With this button you can point to an object and click on it to receive a short help screen about the object. Notice how the mouse pointer changes shape to resemble the button's picture.

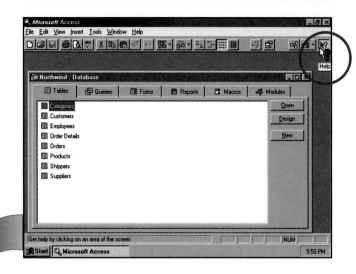

NOTE ▼

You can also access context-sensitive help at any time by pressing the key. Access displays the appropriate Help screen for the procedure or object with which you are currently working.

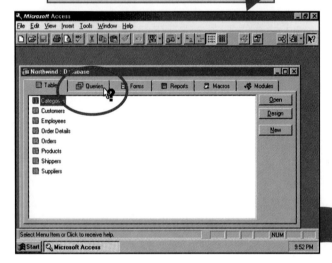

2 Move the mouse pointer to the **Queries** tab on the Database window.

WHY WORRY?

If you do not find the information that you seek with one help method, try another. You can quickly jump from one method to another using the Help dialog tab buttons and the Help toolbar button.

3 Click the question mark mouse pointer on the Queries tab. You see a short information screen about using the Queries tab. Press the **Esc** key or click the mouse once again, and the help screen disappears from your screen. ■

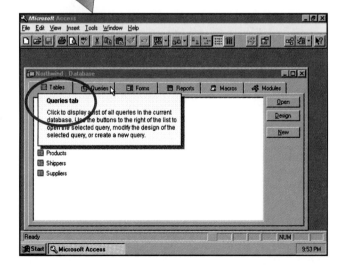

Exiting Access for Windows 95

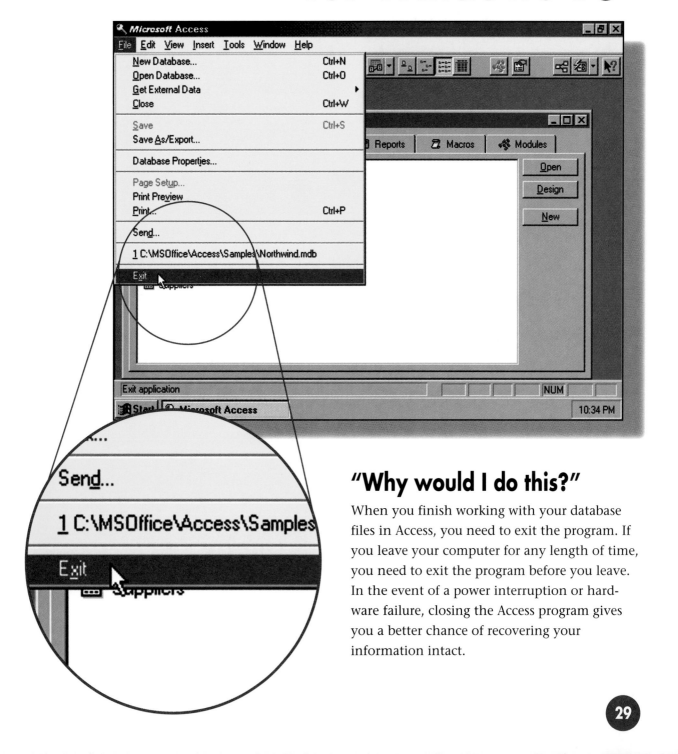

"Why would I do this?"

When you finish working with your database files in Access, you need to exit the program. If you leave your computer for any length of time, you need to exit the program before you leave. In the event of a power interruption or hardware failure, closing the Access program gives you a better chance of recovering your information intact.

1 Open the **File** menu. You see the menu appear with its list of options.

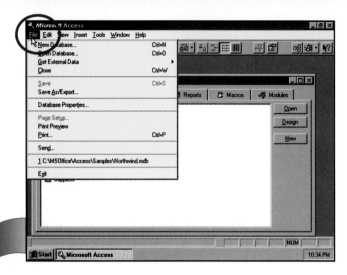

> **NOTE** ▼
>
> You can also exit from the Access program by clicking the Close button in the upper right-hand corner of the Access window, or by pressing the Alt+F4 key combination.

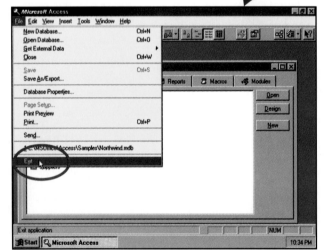

2 Choose the **Exit** option at the bottom of the File menu. Access closes and returns you to the Windows 95 desktop. ■

> **WHY WORRY?**
>
> If you inadvertently select the File command, and you are not ready to exit from Access, press the Esc key. This closes the menu. You can also click the mouse anywhere on the desktop—outside of the menu list and toolbar—to close the menu.

Creating a Shortcut for Access on Your Desktop

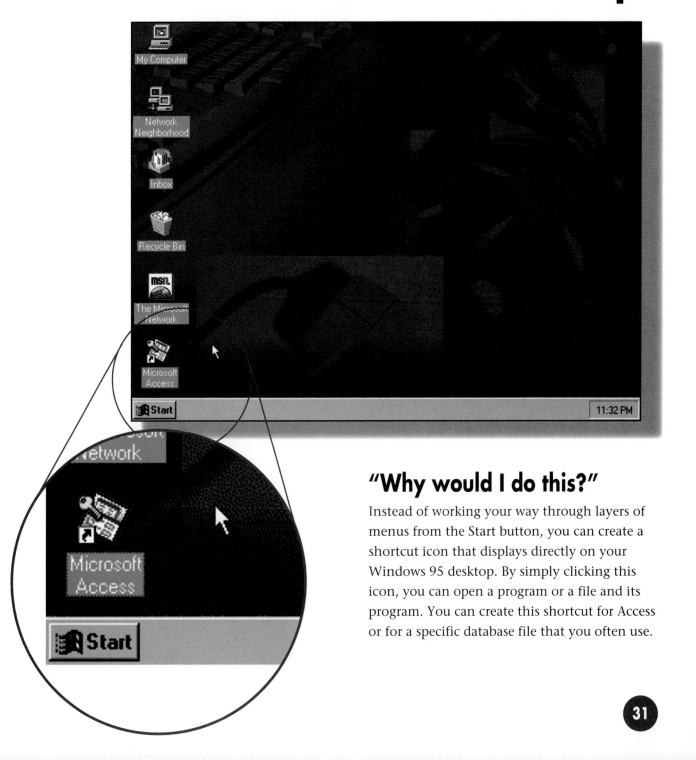

"Why would I do this?"

Instead of working your way through layers of menus from the Start button, you can create a shortcut icon that displays directly on your Windows 95 desktop. By simply clicking this icon, you can open a program or a file and its program. You can create this shortcut for Access or for a specific database file that you often use.

1 Double-click the **My Computer** icon on your Windows 95 desktop. You see a window that displays icons for each of the drives that you have on your computer as well as a Control Panel and Printers icon.

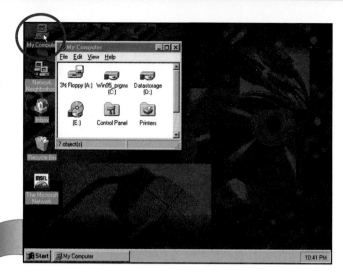

2 Select and double-click the drive icon for the hard disk drive that contains the Access program. You generally find that the program is on the hard disk labeled C:. A window that shows the folders for the selected drive appears.

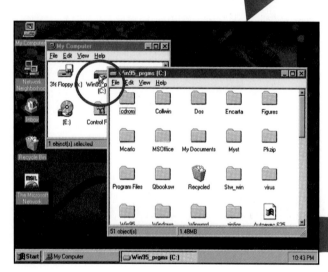

3 Choose and double-click the folder that contains the Access program or folder. In this example, it is the **MSOffice** folder. The MSOffice window appears with its folders.

WHY WORRY?

If you do not find the file you want, you can always use the Windows Explorer to help you find the Access program file.

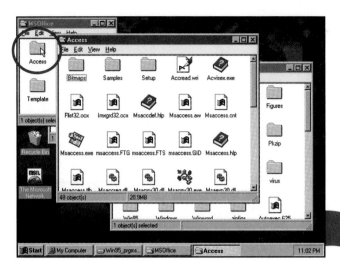

4 Double-click **Access** in the MSOffice window to view the contents of this folder.

5 You now see the Access window; it contains several additional folders and many program icons. The icon for the Access program file is a gold key on a form labeled **Msaccess.exe**. Select this file by clicking it once.

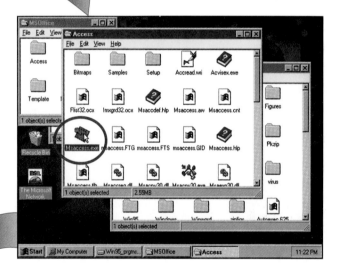

6 Drag the Access icon from the window and drop it on the blank space above the Start button. You now see a new icon, **Shortcut to Msaccess.exe**.

7 Close each of the open windows using each window's **Close** button. You now see your Access shortcut icon on the Windows 95 desktop. It doesn't matter in what order you close the windows.

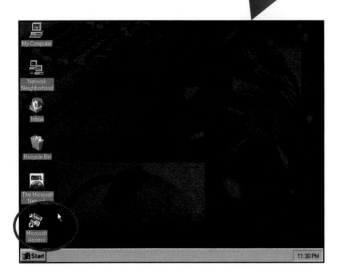

8 Place the mouse pointer inside the shortcut label box and click twice (click two times; do not double-click). Now type **Microsoft Access** as the new label and then click outside the label box. This is the new label for this shortcut. ■

NOTE ▼

The next time you are ready to start Access, simply double-click your short-cut icon. A small arrow in the lower-left corner of the icon indicates that the icon is a shortcut.

PART II

Using a Database

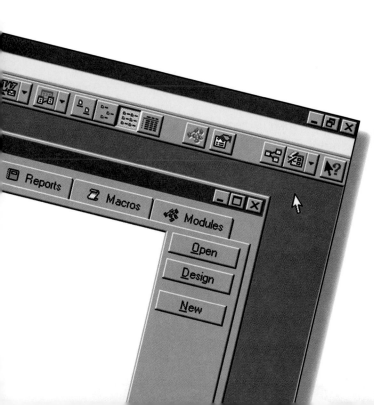

An Access table holds any information that you want to record. For example, you can create a Customer table that contains information related to your customers and the orders they place.

A table contains all of the information about a specific subject. Each row of a table contains an individual *record*. Every record in a table is unique; this is one of the greatest powers of a database. In the case of the Customer table, each record holds all of the information about a single customer.

Each record is made up of elements called *fields*. Each field describes a unique part of the record. In the case of the Customer table there are fields for: Customer ID, Customer Name, Address, City, State, and ZIP Code.

You format a field to control the type of information that it contains. For example, you can format the Quantity field in the Line Items table to accept only numbers. This prevents you from accidentally entering *ABC* into this field. You can also format a field to accept only dates, or text of a specified length.

Depending on your type of business, you might need to add other fields such as Phone Number and Fax Number. As you add customers, and these customers place additional orders, the table begins to grow faster and faster. As the table grows, Access has to sift through larger amounts of data for customer or order information. The biggest problem with this form of database is that for each customer who conducts repeat business with you the database requires you to duplicate the data about the customer for each new order. This often leads to inaccurate information because of typos and other data entry errors. In addition, duplicate records cause your table to grow quickly, requiring more and more of your precious disk space.

The idea behind a relational database such as Access is to remove the need for duplicate information. A table holds a specific type of data, such as customer name and address, or product details. Information in one table is then related to information in another table. If for some reason you need to edit data, such as a customer's address, you only have to perform this task in one place—not for each line in the customer's address that occurs in the table.

The table below shows four tables that each contain information about a specific subject. The tables are then related through a field. The Customer table is related to the Invoice table because each invoice identifies a customer with the Customer ID field. When relating tables in this way, each customer must have a unique Customer ID, otherwise you can have an invoice that has a link to more than one customer. Most tables that you create in Access use a *primary key* field as a unique identifying field. A primary key field by definition cannot have a duplicate value anywhere in the table. The easiest way to link two tables together is to use the primary key field of one table as a *foreign key* in the second table. In the table below, the Customer table uses the Customer ID field as its primary key, while the Invoice table uses this same field as a foreign key to create a relationship between the tables.

Customer	Invoice	Line Items	Inventory
Customer ID	Invoice Number	Invoice Number	Item Code
Customer Name	Customer ID	Item Code	Item Description
Address	Invoice Date	Unit Price	Supplier
City		Quantity Ordered	Quantity On Hand
State			Unit Cost
Zip Code			

This table contains information in fields such as Customer Name, Address, Invoice Number, Invoice Date, Item Sold, Quantity Sold, and Price. Each of these tables contains fields that are unique to that table and a field that provides a link to at least one other table. The arrows indicate the linking fields between the four tables. By using tables that are related to each other through a linking field, you can build a well-designed, efficient database. Dividing your information into groups or subjects allows you to condense the sheer quantity of information to a small fraction of what a single table requires and helps to ensure that information is not duplicated.

As you begin the process of designing your own database, take the time to determine your information needs. Ask yourself, for example, what data you need to include. Attention to the initial design of your database pays off by minimizing corrections later. A simple method to begin the design process is to lay out your database on paper. Draw a block for each subject you need to keep information on: Customers, Products, and Orders. Then list each specific part of the subject and draw lines between each block to indicate which piece of information links them together. This part introduces you to the essential elements that go into designing and creating a table.

Creating a New Database

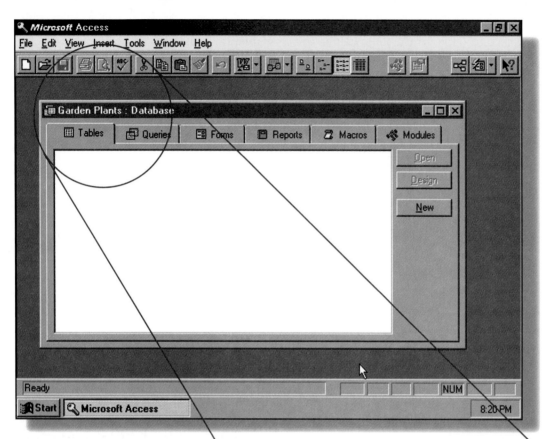

"Why would I do this?"

Before you can begin to build any of the objects that make up your database, you must create the file that holds the objects. The database file is the container in which your information lives. As you continue to develop your database into the powerful tool that can perform the functions you require of it, your database file grows. Except under certain circumstances, this file contains all of the objects that compose your database.

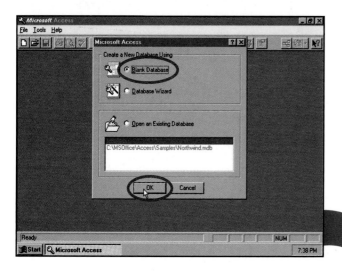

1 Double-click the **Access** shortcut button to start the program. In the Microsoft Access dialog box that appears, select the **Blank Database** option button. Click **OK**.

> **NOTE** ▼
>
> If Access is already open, you can create a new database file by selecting File, New Database from the menu bar, or using the keyboard shortcut Ctrl+N.

2 You use the File New Database dialog box that appears to name your new file and select the location for Access to store it. Access automatically names your database *db1*. Unless you plan to use only a single database file, you want to provide your database files with descriptive names.

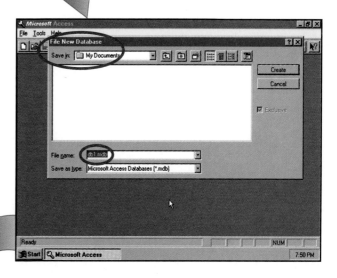

3 You first choose the location for your new database file. The default location for all new documents is the My Documents folder. The NWIND database file is in the Samples folder. Click the **Create New Folder** button to create a new folder in which to save your database file.

4 Type **Plant Files** and press the **OK** button. This folder is a subfolder of the My Documents folder. This enables you to categorize the documents that you frequently use into groups.

WHY WORRY?

You can always move a file to a different folder later if the one in which you place it is not convenient.

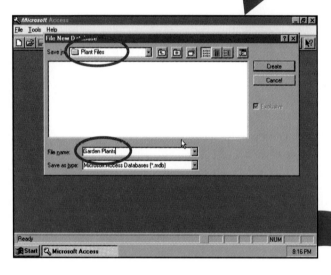

5 Double-click the folder **Plant Files**. In the File name text box, type **Garden Plants** as the name for your new file.

6 Click the **Create** button. Access creates the database file Garden Plants, places it in the folder Plant Files, and opens the new file. All of the object windows that appear in the Database window are blank because this is a new database. ■

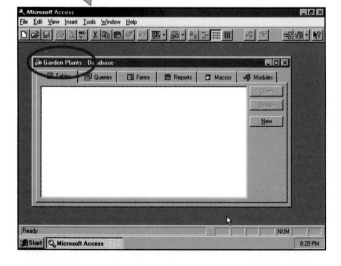

Using a Table Wizard

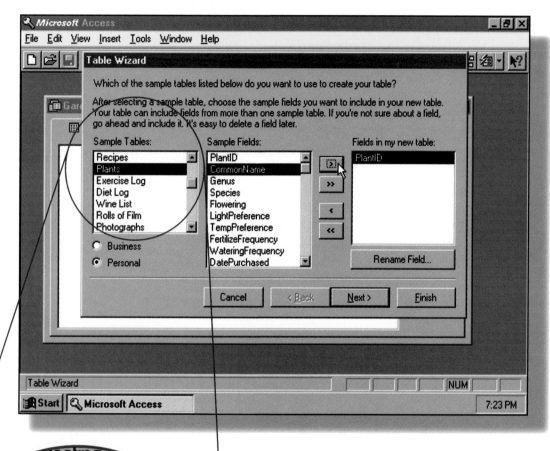

"Why would I do this?"

Now that you have a file where you can place the database objects, such as tables, you must build the tables in which you store your information. The Table Wizard is a special Access function that helps you build a table by asking you a series of questions with dialog boxes.

1 Before you can add a table to a database you must open the database file by clicking the **Open Database** button on the toolbar and selecting the database file from the Open dialog box. Choose the file **Garden Plants** in the **Plant Files** folder. Click the **Open** button to open the file.

NOTE ▼

The Database window displays a listing of all the available tables in the list box. The list box is empty now because there are no tables.

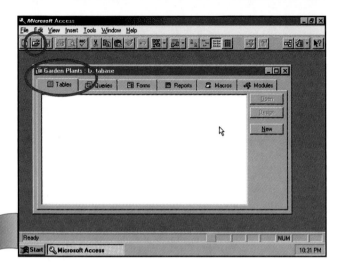

2 Click the **New** button on the Database window. It is the only active button available to you on the Database window at this time. This opens the New Table dialog box.

NOTE ▼

You can also press Alt+N, or select Insert, Table, to activate the New Table dialog box.

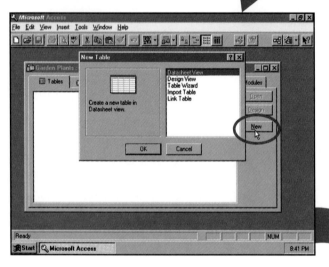

3 Select the **Table Wizard** option from the list box and click the **OK** button. You can use the Table Wizard to help you set up a complete or partial database table. You can choose from 77 Business category and 44 Personal category tables.

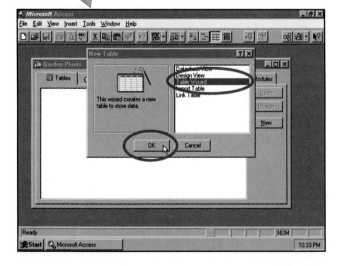

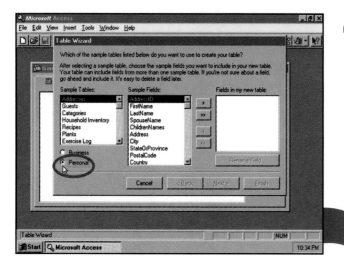

4 Click the **Personal** option button. Access displays the Personal category list of tables in the Sample Tables list box.

> **NOTE** ▼
>
> To view the available options for predefined tables, scroll up and down both the Business and Personal lists in the Sample Tables list box. The Sample Fields list box shows the list of field names for the predefined table you select in the Sample Tables list box.

5 Scroll down the Sample Tables list box until you see the table name **Plants**. Select it by clicking the name once. You now see the list of predefined fields in the Sample Fields list box.

> **WHY WORRY?**
>
> If you do not see a field in the Sample Fields list box for a specific type of information that you want to collect, you can redesign the table and add this field later.

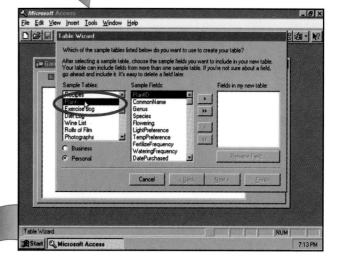

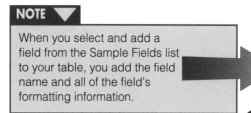

6 Select the **PlantID** field from the Sample fields list box. This is the first field that you include in the new table. Select the field by clicking it once. When you select a field, Access highlights it.

> **NOTE** ▼
>
> When you select and add a field from the Sample Fields list to your table, you add the field name and all of the field's formatting information.

45

7 Click the **>** button. You see Access copy the selected field name to the Fields in my new table list box. Repeat steps 6 and 7 for each field that you want to include in your new table. Add these fields to the new table list box: CommonName, Genus, Species, Flowering, LightPreference, FertilizeFrequency, WateringFrequency, DatePurchased, PlacePurchased, DatePlanted, and Notes.

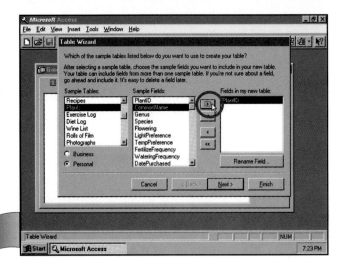

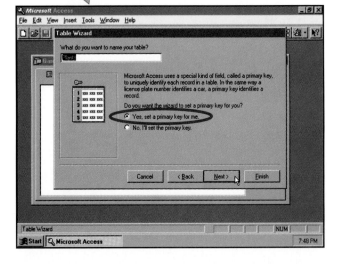

8 Select the **Notes** field name in the Fields in my new table list box and click the **Rename Field** button. In the Rename Field dialog box, type the name **Remarks** in the text box and click the **OK** button. Access inserts the new field name.

NOTE ▼

If you want to include all of the fields shown in the Sample Fields list box, click the **>>** instead of the **>** button. With this button you can copy all of the fields at one time, instead of one-by-one.

9 Click the **Next>** button. You use this dialog box to change the default name for a table and manually select a primary key for your table. Simply type a new name into the text box to change it. Select the **Next>** button to move to the next dialog box.

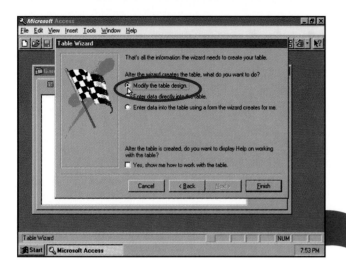

10 The final Table Wizard dialog box appears. Select the **Modify the table design** option button to open your table in the Table Design view and make further changes to the table design.

WHY WORRY?

You can edit your table design at any time. Select the table from the list in the Database window and click the Design button.

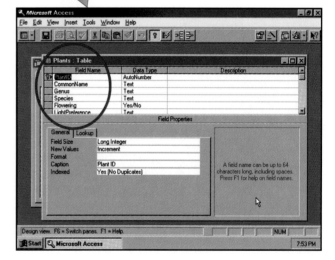

11 Click the **Finish** button. Access completes your table and opens it in the Table Design view. This is the same window that you use to create a table without the help of the Table Wizard. ■

NOTE ▼

Select the Enter data directly into the table option button to open the new table and enter information into it; or, select Enter data into the table using a form the wizard creates to enter data into the table. If you want Access to show you how to use your table, click on the Yes, show me how to work with the table check box.

Adding a New Field

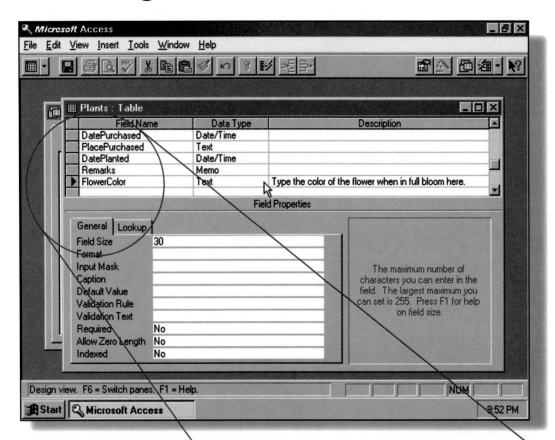

"Why would I do this?"

Often you find that the predefined tables the Table Wizard creates do not include a field for a specific piece of information that you want to gather. In order to correct this problem, you must use the Table Design view option and add this field manually. When you add fields, Access requires you to provide a name and formatting information for the field name. Enter a field name that describes the type of information you plan to store in the field.

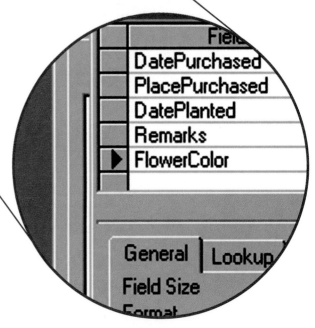

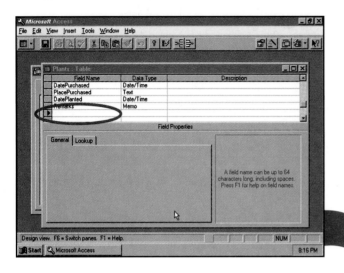

1 Press the down-arrow key on your keyboard until you enter the first blank row in the Field Name column. This is where you enter your new field name.

2 Type **FlowerColor** in the blank row of the Field Name column. Field names can be a maximum of 64 characters long. You can use any combination of letters, numbers, spaces, and other characters. You can't include periods (.), exclamation points (!), grave accent (`), brackets ([or]), or spaces at the beginning of the field name.

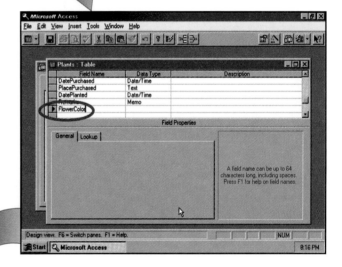

3 Press the **Enter** key to move to the Data Type column. Click the **arrow** button in the Data Type field. This displays a drop-down list of available options. Select the **Text** option for your new field. This is the default data type option.

4 Press the **Enter** key once again to move to the next column, Description. Type **Type the color of the flower when in full bloom here.** This is the descriptive text for the FlowerColor field.

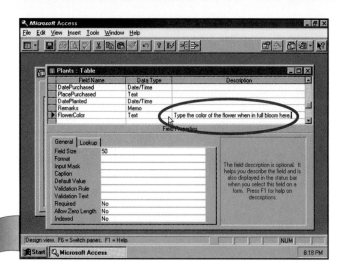

NOTE ▼

Using descriptions for fields is optional. Access displays these descriptions in the status bar when the user enters field information. You can always change the description if you find that it doesn't meet your information needs.

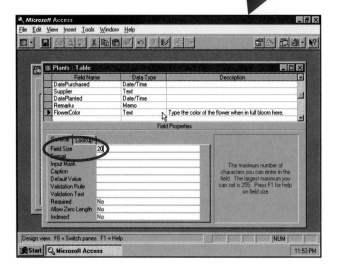

5 Press **F6** to switch to the lower pane of this window. You now see the cursor in the Field Size property text box. The Field Size property text box enables you to specify the length of the field. Type **20**. The maximum length for a text field is 255 characters; the default setting is 50 characters. ∎

NOTE ▼

Don't arbitrarily set a text field to 255 characters. If you set a large number for the field size, Access uses that number to allocate memory and disk storage requirements. The fewer characters you set for the field size, the less memory and disk space the field takes up.

Working with Number Fields

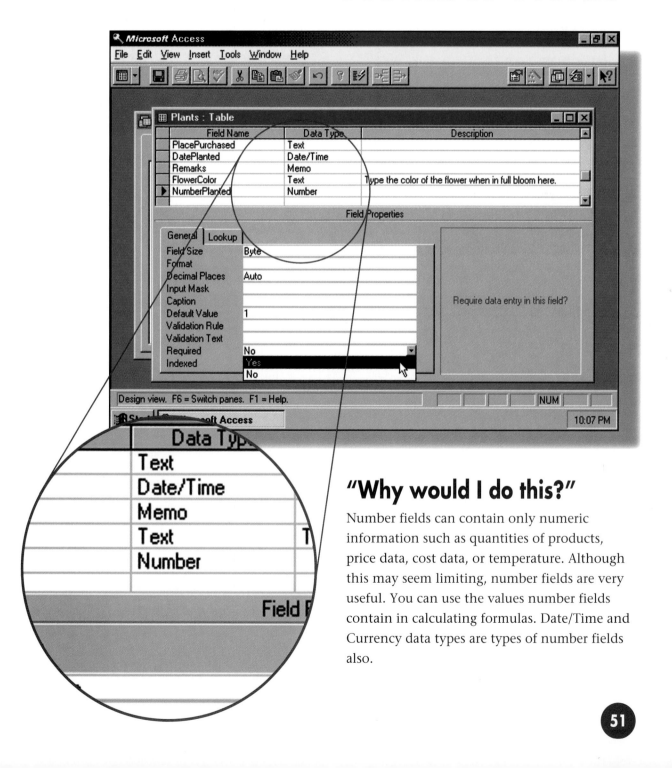

"Why would I do this?"

Number fields can contain only numeric information such as quantities of products, price data, cost data, or temperature. Although this may seem limiting, number fields are very useful. You can use the values number fields contain in calculating formulas. Date/Time and Currency data types are types of number fields also.

1 Move the cursor to the next blank row in the Field Name column by clicking it with the mouse pointer. Type **NumberPlanted** and press the **Enter** key.

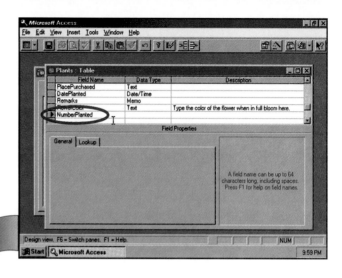

NOTE ▼

The Byte option of the Field Size property enables you to enter any positive whole number between 0 and 255. For help using the Field Size property, press the F1 key.

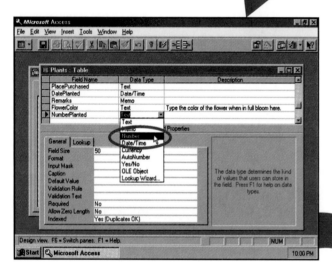

2 Press the **Enter** or **Tab** key moving to the Data Type column. Click the arrow button in the Data Type column to display the drop-down list. Select the **Number** data type.

NOTE ▼

For a field that contains only dates and/or times, select the Date/Time data type. A date field holds any date from January 1, 100 to December 31, 9999. Choose the Currency data type for a field that contains monetary amounts.

3 Press **F6**, or click the Field Size text box, and click the arrow button to display the drop-down list. Click the **Byte** option. For number fields, the Field Size property enables you to select the type of number and range of numbers that the user enters into this field.

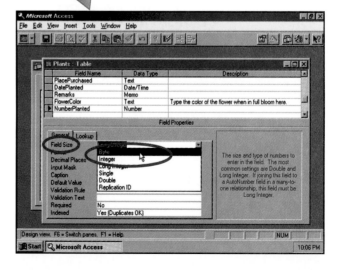

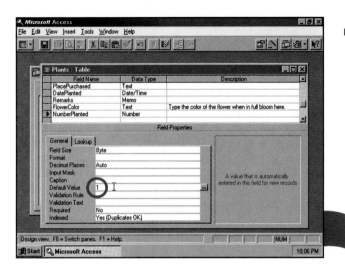

4 Click the **Default Value** text box and type the number **1**. This becomes the default value that Access enters into this field in your table. You can always override a default value by typing in a different value.

5 Move down to the **Required** text box. Click the **arrow** button and select the **Yes** option. This property setting requires that you enter a value into the field before you can update and save a record. ■

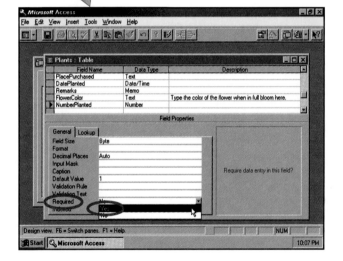

WHY WORRY?

Remember, you can go back and change a value in a table if you entered the wrong number, or forgot to enter a number, allowing Access to fill in the default value.

Using Yes/No Fields

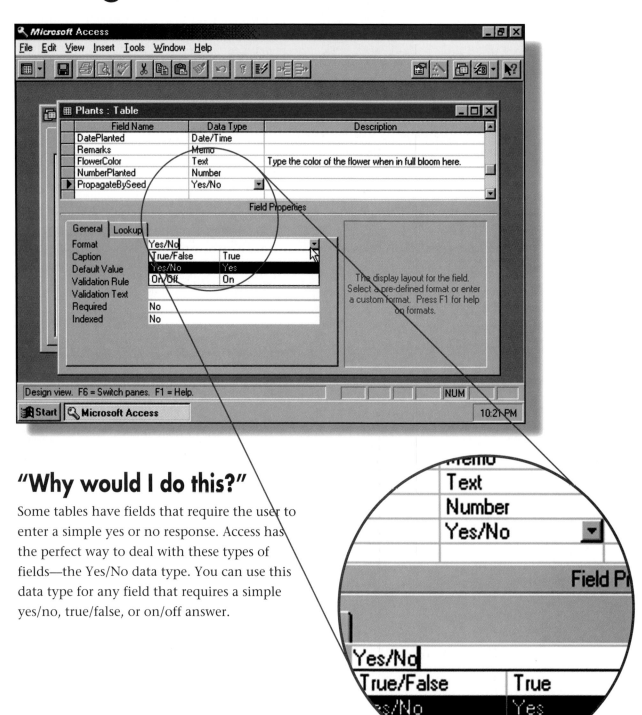

"Why would I do this?"

Some tables have fields that require the user to enter a simple yes or no response. Access has the perfect way to deal with these types of fields—the Yes/No data type. You can use this data type for any field that requires a simple yes/no, true/false, or on/off answer.

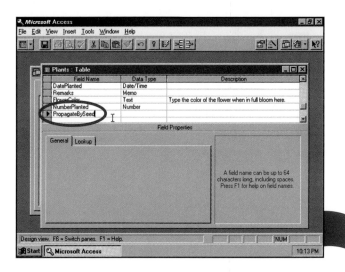

1 Move the cursor to the next blank field row in the Field Name column. Type the field name **PropagateBySeed** and press the **Enter** key.

WHY WORRY?

By using a Yes/No type of field, you can help to eliminate data entry errors by requiring users to select only one of two responses to a field.

2 Move to the Data Type column and click the arrow button to select the **Yes/No** option from the drop-down list.

NOTE ▼

If you know the name of the data type that you want to select from a drop-down list, you can also type in the first letter or two of the data type. Access fills in the rest for you. For example, if you type in the letter Y, Access fills in Yes/No.

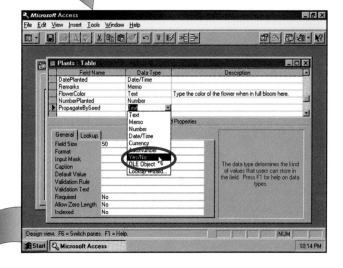

3 In the Field Properties area, click the **Format** option and click the **arrow** button. Select the **Yes/No** option. (These are the most appropriate answers for the user to give for this particular field.)

NOTE ▼

You can access a drop-down list from your keyboard by pressing the Alt+down-arrow key combination. Use the up- and down-arrow keys to select a specific option.

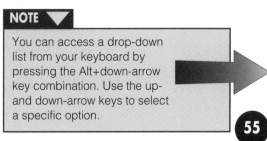

Saving the New Table Definition

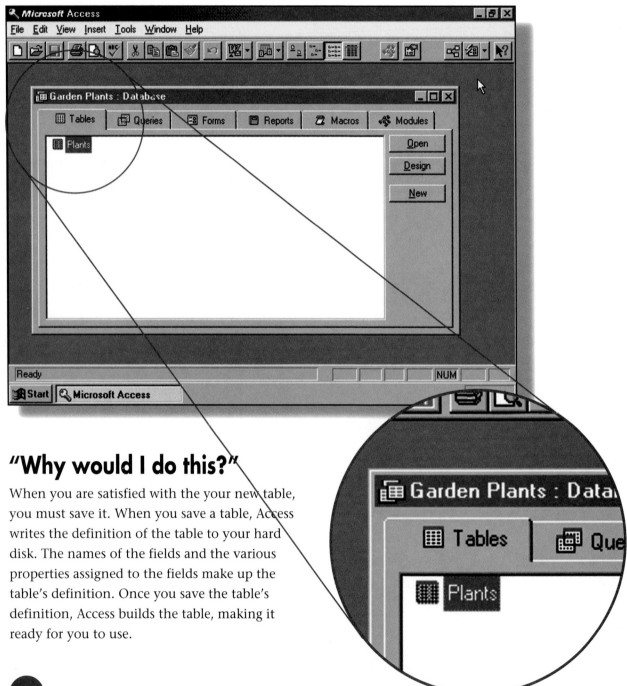

"Why would I do this?"

When you are satisfied with the your new table, you must save it. When you save a table, Access writes the definition of the table to your hard disk. The names of the fields and the various properties assigned to the fields make up the table's definition. Once you save the table's definition, Access builds the table, making it ready for you to use.

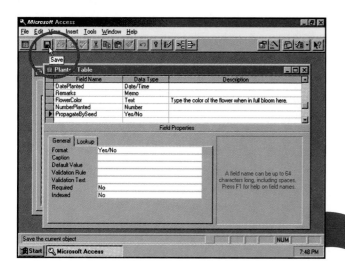

1 Click the **Save** button on the toolbar. The Table Wizard saves the table when you originally finish it, but you must save the changes you make to the original table definition. If you watch the status bar closely, you see different messages displayed as Access completes each procedure necessary for saving your table.

2 You can also save a table definition by choosing **Save** from the **File** menu, or using the keyboard combination **Ctrl+S**.

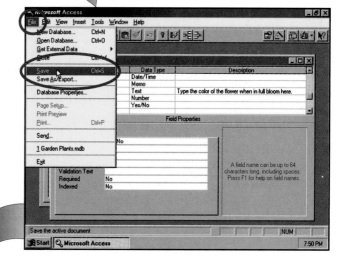

WHY WORRY?

If you are not finished with your changes to the table definition, you can continue to add new fields or change field properties and simply save the edited definition again.

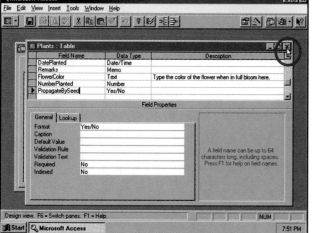

3 Click the **Close** button in the upper right corner of the Table Design view window (not the Access program window). You now see the new table, Plants, in the Tables list. ∎

NOTE ▼

If you create a table from scratch, you see a dialog box requesting you to enter a name for the table. Since you created this table with the help of the Table Wizard, it already has a name.

TASK 15

Opening a Table

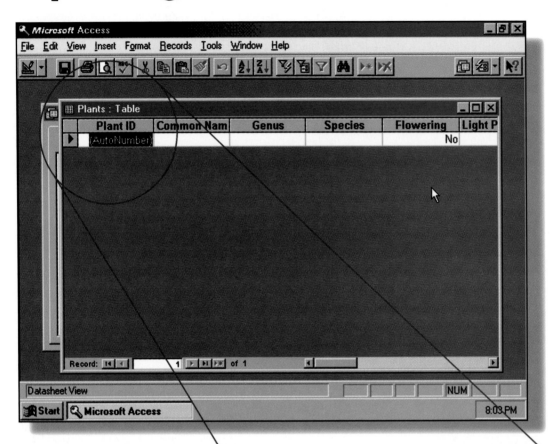

"Why would I do this?"

Once you create a table and its definition, you're ready to start entering data into it. An unopened table is similar to an unopened ledger or order pad: you can't work with either one until you open it.

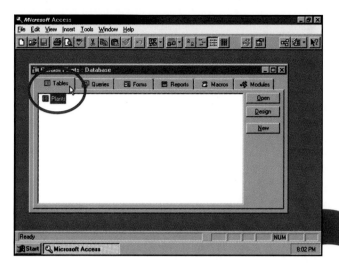

1 Click the **Tables** tab on the Database window to display the Table list. You see the list of available tables. Select a table from the list by clicking its name or pressing the up- or down-arrow keys until the name of the table you want to select is highlighted.

2 Click the **Open** button on the Database window.

> **NOTE** ▼
>
> Remember, you can use the keyboard shortcut Alt+O to open the selected table, or simply double-click the table icon.

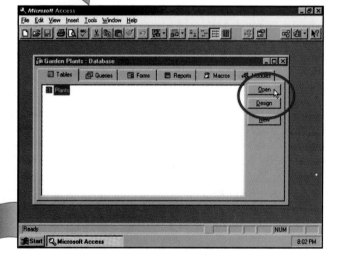

3 The Plants table appears in datasheet view. ■

59

Changing a Field Name

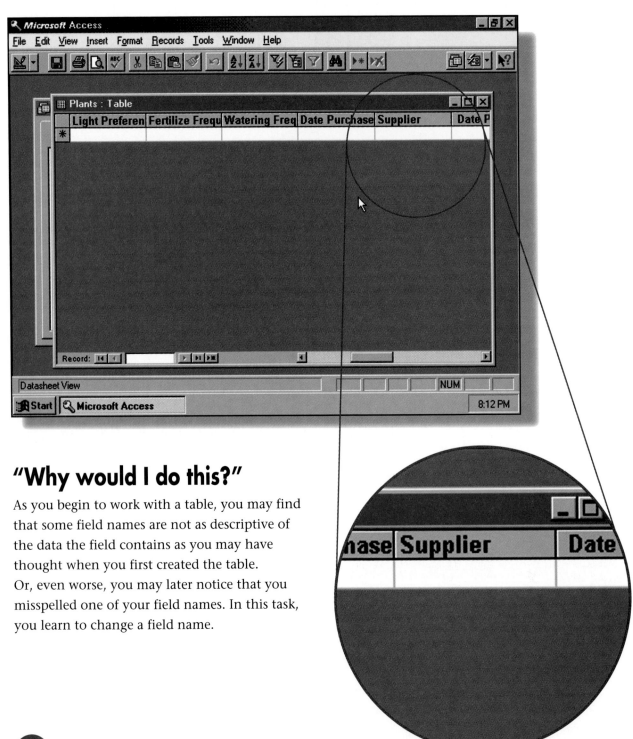

"Why would I do this?"

As you begin to work with a table, you may find that some field names are not as descriptive of the data the field contains as you may have thought when you first created the table. Or, even worse, you may later notice that you misspelled one of your field names. In this task, you learn to change a field name.

1 Be sure that you select the **Tables** tab on the Database window. Double-click the **Plants** table to open it.

NOTE ▼

Remember, you can also open a table by selecting it and clicking the Open button, or pressing the keyboard combination Alt+O.

2 Click the right scroll bar button at the bottom of the table window until you see the field **Place Purchased** display.

WHY WORRY?

If you scroll too far, simply click the left scroll bar button to bring the field back in view. It doesn't matter if the field is in the middle of the window or to one side or the other.

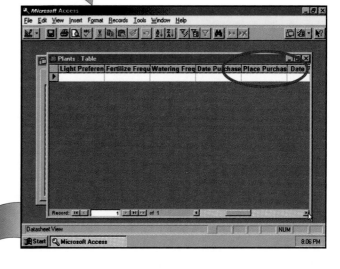

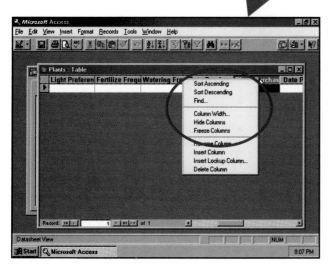

3 Move the mouse pointer to the **Place Purchased** column header and click the right mouse button.

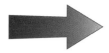

4 Select the **Rename Column** option from the shortcut menu that displays and click once. You now see the selected field name in the column header and the blinking editing cursor at the beginning of the field name. Type **Supplier** as the new field name.

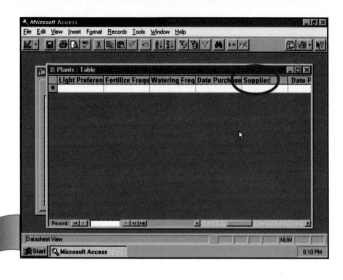

5 To see that the table definition contains this field name change, click the **Table View** button on the toolbar. When you can see the table in the Table Design view window, scroll down the field list until you see the new field name Supplier.

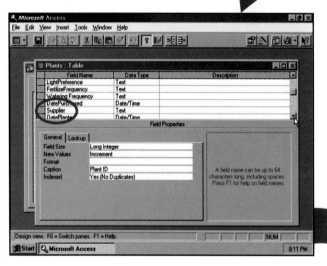

6 Click the **Save** button to save the revised table definition. To close the table, click the **Close** button. ■

WHY WORRY?

If you forget to save the revised table definition, but you go ahead and click the Close button, Access displays a dialog box asking you if you want to save your changes before you close the table.

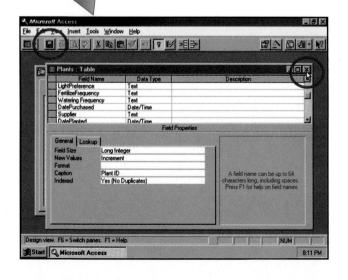

Moving a Field within a Table

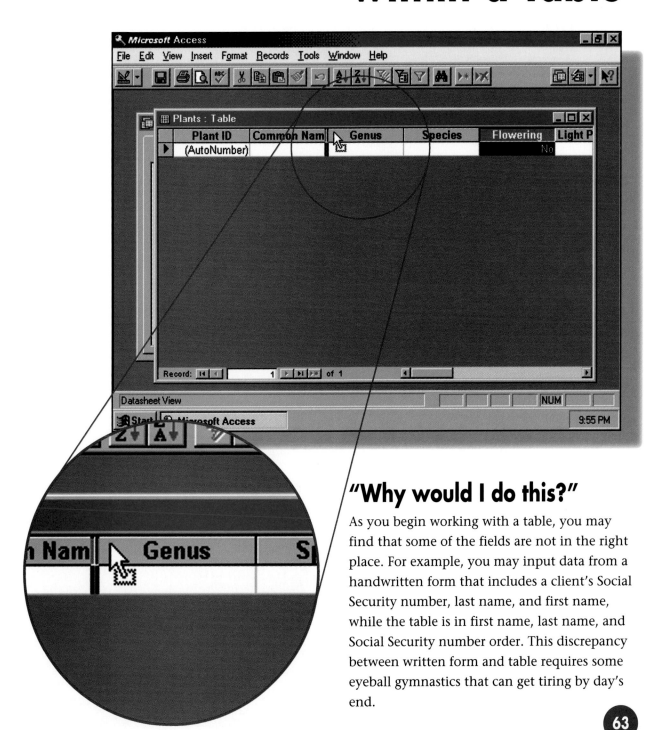

"Why would I do this?"

As you begin working with a table, you may find that some of the fields are not in the right place. For example, you may input data from a handwritten form that includes a client's Social Security number, last name, and first name, while the table is in first name, last name, and Social Security number order. This discrepancy between written form and table requires some eyeball gymnastics that can get tiring by day's end.

1 Open the **Plants** table by selecting the table in the Database window. Click the **Open** button. The table opens in the normal Datasheet view.

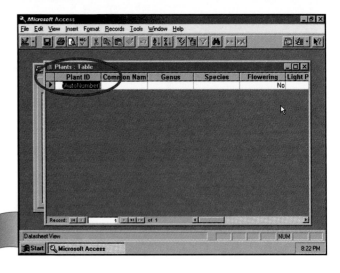

2 Select the column header **Flowering** by clicking on it once. Notice that Access highlights the entire column.

NOTE ▼

> To drag an object, select it by pressing and holding the left mouse button as you move the mouse pointer to the object's new location. Here you see a stylized object move along with the mouse pointer.

3 Now click and drag the field to the left of the Genus field, where you see a thick vertical bar showing the field's new location between the Common Name and Genus fields.

NOTE ▼

> The field name Common Name is cut off because the field is simply not wide enough to display the field's entire name. Double-clicking the right edge of the column header button automatically widens the column to best fit the name.

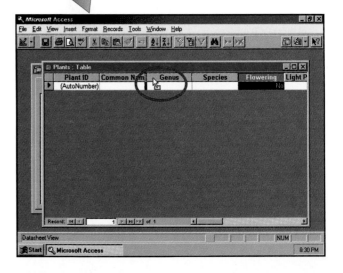

64

4 Set the field in place by releasing the mouse button. You save this field in its new position by clicking the **Save** button. If you don't save the table's new format now, Access asks you if you want to save the new settings when you close the table.

5 If you don't save the new table format, it reverts back to its original format. Click the **Close** button and do not save the new table format by clicking the **No** button. ■

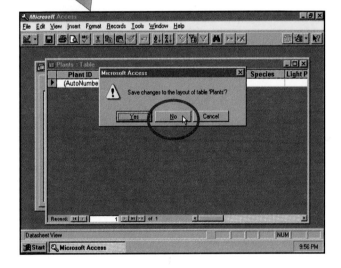

WHY WORRY?

You can change the order of the columns in any table at any time. Changing the column order does not affect any of the information the table contains, nor does it affect any other object that is based on the table.

Inserting a Field

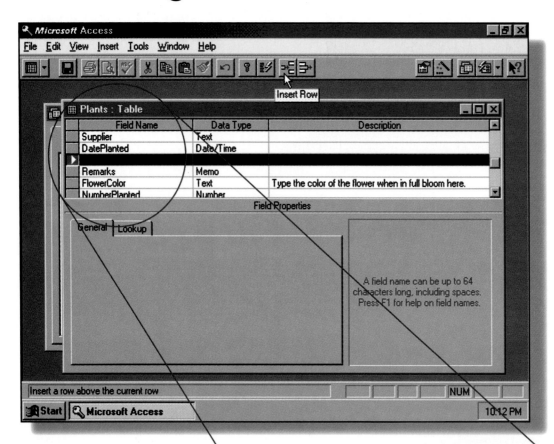

"Why would I do this?"

You may find that you need to store additional
information in a table. You can add another
field to your table definition and move the
column to a more appropriate position in the
table, or insert a blank line into your table
definition and enter the new field information—saving yourself several extra steps.

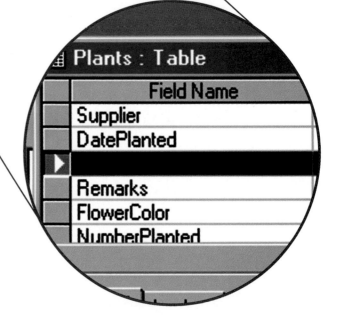

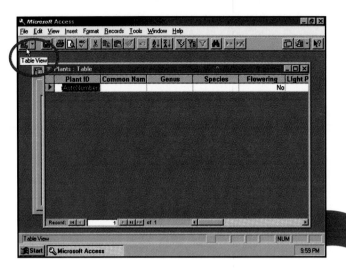

1 Open the **Plants** table if it is not already on-screen. Move the mouse pointer to the **Table View** button on the toolbar and click it once. You see the table switch from Datasheet view to Table Design view.

2 When you insert a field into the table definition you must move the row selector to the field name located below the newly inserted field. Scroll through the field list until you see the field Remarks. Click the row selector button beside it to select the field.

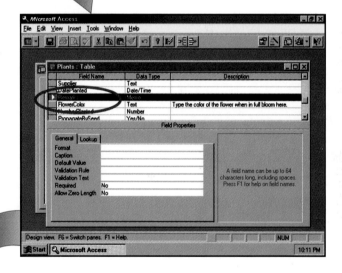

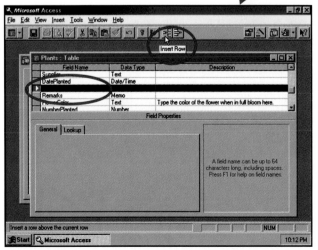

3 Move the mouse pointer to the **Insert Row** button and click it once. Access inserts the field, and you see a blank row above the selected field.

NOTE ▼

You can delete a row by selecting it and clicking the Delete Row button.

4 Click the mouse pointer in the **Field Name** column of the new row. Type **Location** as the new field name in the Field Name column.

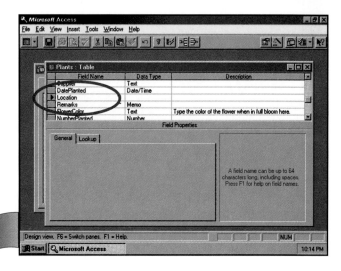

5 Press the **Tab** key and select **Text** for the Data Type for the new field. Now is the time to make any changes to the field's properties in the lower pane of this window.

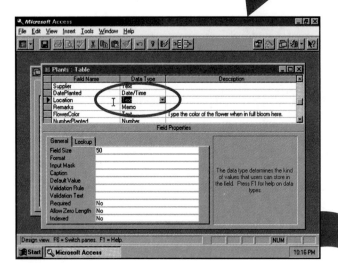

WHY WORRY?

If you decide that you do not want to use this field, select the No button when Access prompts you to save your new changes to this table, or simply delete the new field with the Delete Row button.

6 Click the **Save** button to save the table's new definition, and click the **Table View** button to return to the Datasheet view. You can see the new field by scrolling toward the right edge of the table. ∎

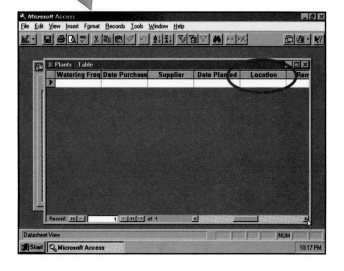

Deleting a Field

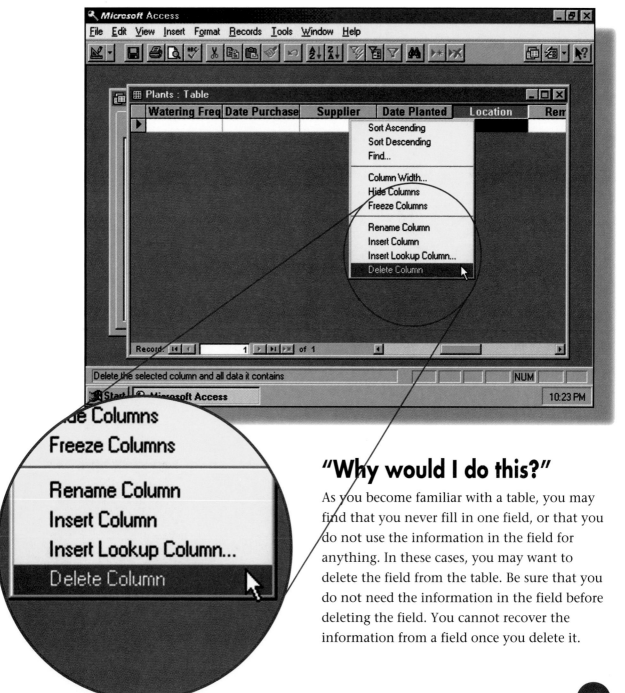

"Why would I do this?"

As you become familiar with a table, you may find that you never fill in one field, or that you do not use the information in the field for anything. In these cases, you may want to delete the field from the table. Be sure that you do not need the information in the field before deleting the field. You cannot recover the information from a field once you delete it.

1 Open the **Plants** table in the Datasheet view. Scroll through the table toward its right edge until you see the field **Location**. Select the field by clicking the column header button.

> **NOTE**
>
> After you save the new table definition, you cannot recover any of the field's information, so be sure you have selected the correct field.

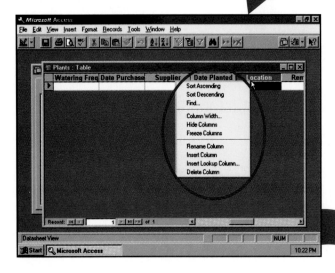

2 Click the right mouse button to display the shortcut menu.

3 Select the **Delete Column** option from the shortcut menu. Access deletes the column from the table. ■

> **WHY WORRY?**
>
> If you are not absolutely positive you want to delete a field, you can save a copy of the table with the Copy and Paste commands. Just give the copy of the table a new name.

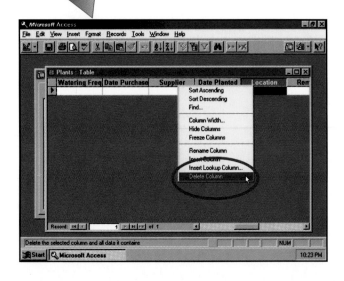

Building a Table from Scratch

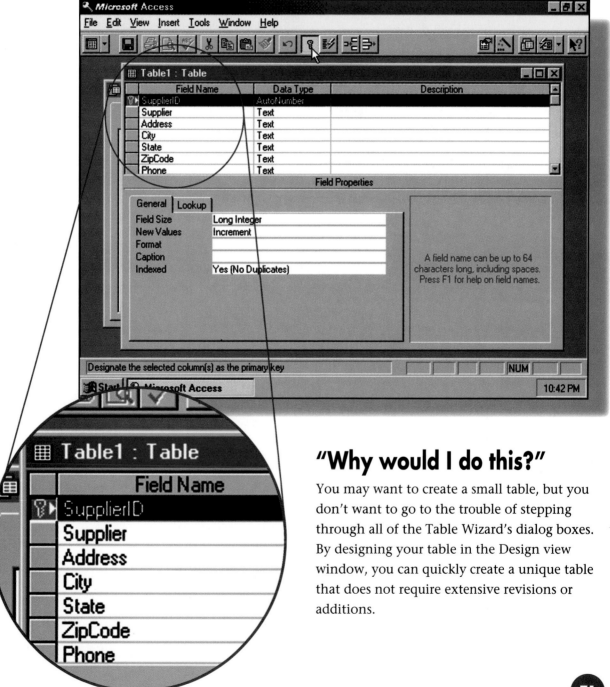

"Why would I do this?"

You may want to create a small table, but you don't want to go to the trouble of stepping through all of the Table Wizard's dialog boxes. By designing your table in the Design view window, you can quickly create a unique table that does not require extensive revisions or additions.

1 Be sure that the **Tables** tab is selected in the Database window. Click the **New** button to display the New Table dialog box. Use this dialog box to choose how to go about building your table.

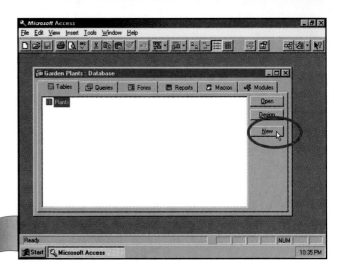

2 Choose the **Design View** option from the list and click the **OK** button. This opens the Table Design view window with a blank field list.

NOTE ▼

Generally, you'll find that it's easier to work with a multiple table database if you include an ID field that uses the AutoNumber data type. One of the secrets of a successful database is to ensure that each record in a table is unique.

3 Type **SupplierID** as the Field Name in the first row. This is the identifying, or *key*, field for this table. Press the **Tab** key and choose **AutoNumber** for the data type. This field ensures that each record has a unique, identifying field.

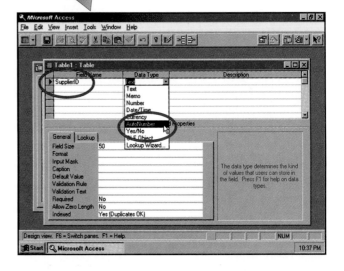

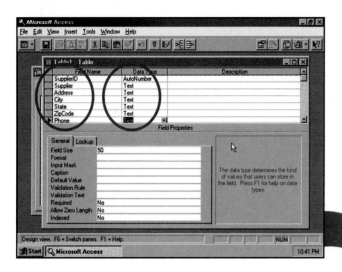

4 Add the following fields in order: **Supplier**, **Address**, **City**, **State**, **ZipCode**, **Phone**. Each field uses the default data type Text.

NOTE ▼

If you notice a typo in one of your field names , simply select the field name and retype it. Editing the field name does not affect the field properties or data type that you set for the field.

5 Type **CatalogOnly** in the Field Name column to add one last field. Use the data type **Yes/No**.

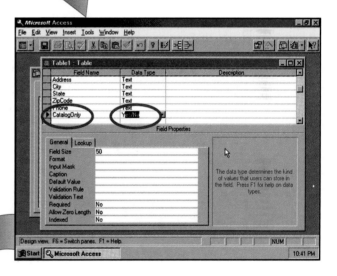

6 Scroll back to the beginning of the field list to the **SupplierID** field and click its **row selector** button. This selects the entire row and ensures that you selected the correct field.

WHY WORRY?

If you miss with the mouse and select the wrong row, just move the mouse pointer and click again.

7 Move the mouse pointer to the **Primary Key** button on the toolbar and click it once. You see a small key symbol, like the one that appears on the Primary Key button face, displayed on the SupplierID's row selector button. By setting this field as the primary key, you can link it to a foreign key in another table.

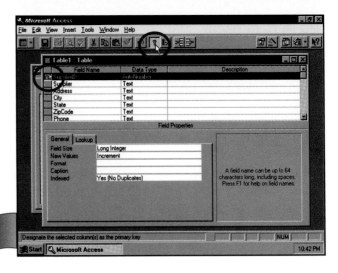

8 After you complete the table, click the **Save** button on the toolbar. This opens the Save As dialog box. Type **Plant Suppliers** into the text box, overwriting the default name of Table1.

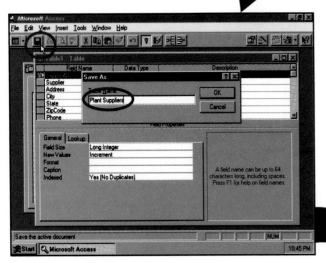

9 Click the **OK** button to save the new table definition, then click the **Close** button on the Table Design view window. Access adds your new table to the Database window. ∎

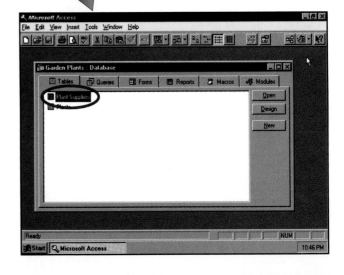

PART III
Entering and Editing Data

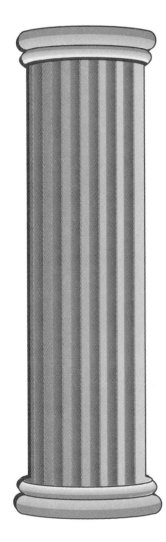

N ow that you have your database file and two tables for it, you can begin to enter information into the tables. When you add information to a table, you normally enter all of the information for a single record, and then move to the next one. Remember, each row of the table is a single record. You can think of each record as a single, blank sheet of paper. When you fill in the necessary information for the record, turn to the next blank page and enter the next record.

Each distinct piece of the record is in its own field. Each field fills a single line of the paper. As you complete the information for a field, you move to the next line. In the Plants table in Part II, you have fields for Common Name, Genus, Species, and other information related to each plant. The second table, Plant Suppliers, has fields for the supplier's name, address, and other information that relates to each individual business from which you buy your plants. The AutoNumber field numbers each page, or record; in the Plants table, it is PlantID, and, in the Plant Suppliers, it is SupplierID.

In a database file you can easily add information to fields and records, and change the information as necessary. You can change the appearance of your information by using a different font, or by modifying the height of your rows or the width of your columns. If necessary, you can hide selected fields of information from view. This is especially helpful if you work with information of a sensitive nature. For example, suppose you work with personnel or payroll records and want to show a colleague some aspect of the information, but not specific personal data. With Access you can hide the personal data from view.

The most common way you'll enter information in your Access table is by typing it in with the keyboard. After you become more familiar with Windows 95 and Access, you may want to enter information by importing the data from other programs. You can even add pictures to your records.

In addition to storing information in a table, one of the most important functions of using a database is its capability to find and easily update information. With Access, you can use the powerful Find command to search for a specific record or group of records.

Also, unlike your pad of records, each on their own individual page, you can easily sort all of your records in any way that you choose. In the case of the Plants table, you can quickly sort your list of plants by common name, by genus, the date that you planted them, by flower color, or by almost any other field that you want. You can sort records in either an ascending or descending order. An ascending sort order is similar to normal alphabetical order except that numbers come before letters. A descending sort order is the reverse of ascending: letters beginning with Z come first and numbers, ending with the number 0, come last.

In Task 21, "Entering New Information," you need to enter the information the following tables contain. These tables include the information for the records that you use with most of the tasks in this book. Be sure to enter this data exactly as shown, including any typos.

Common Name	Genus	Species	Flowering	Light Preference	Fertilize Frequency	Watering Frequency
Amethyst Flower	Browallia	speciosa	Yes	Shade, Filtered Sun	Weekly	Weekly
Butterfly Bbush	buddleia	alternifolia	Yes	Full Sun	Annually	Keep Dry
Canterbury Bell	Campanula	medium	Yes	Full Sun, Filtered Sun	Monthly	Weekly
Costmary	Chrysanthemum	balsamita	Yes	Full Sun	Monthly	Weekly
Foxglove	Digitalis	purpurea	Yes	Shade, Filtered Sun	Annually	Weekly
Purple Coneflower	Echinacea	purpurea	Yes	Full Sun	Monthly	Weekly
Cranesbill	Geranium	himalayense	Yes	Full Sun	Monthly	Weekly
Lotus	Nelumbo	nucifera	Yes	Full Sun, Filtered Sun	Annually	Keep Wet
catnip	Nepeta	cataria	Yes	Full Sun	Monthly	Weekly
Wormwood	Artemisia	absinthium	Yes	Full Sun	Monthly	Keep Dry

Common Name	Date Purchased	Place Purchased	Date Planted	Remarks	Flower Color	Number Planted	Propagate By Seed
Amethyst Flower	3/1/95	Portland Plants	3/2/95	Annual, may be perennial	Blue	6	Yes
Butterfly Bush	5/15/93	Portland Plants	5/20/93	Perennial	Blue	2	No
Canterbury Bell	12/10/94	Nichol's Plants & Seeds	2/1/95	Biennial	Blue, Pink, White	15	Yes
Costmary	3/15/95	NW Hardy Plants	3/15/95	Perennial	.	3	No
Foxglove	5/1/93	N/A	6/1/93	Biennial, Perennial	Purple	12	Yes
Purple Coneflower	3/1/95	Portland Plants	3/2/95	Perennial	Purple	3	Yes
Cranesbill	6/1/94	St.John's Perennials	6/1/94	Perennial	Lilac	2	No
Lotus	3/15/95	Portland Pond's	3/15/95	Perennial	Pink	2	Yes
catnip	6/1/93	St. John's Perennials	6/1/93	Perennial	White	6	Yes
Wormwood	4/1/94	St. John's Perennials	4/1/94	Perennial	Yellow	1	Yes

Entering New Information

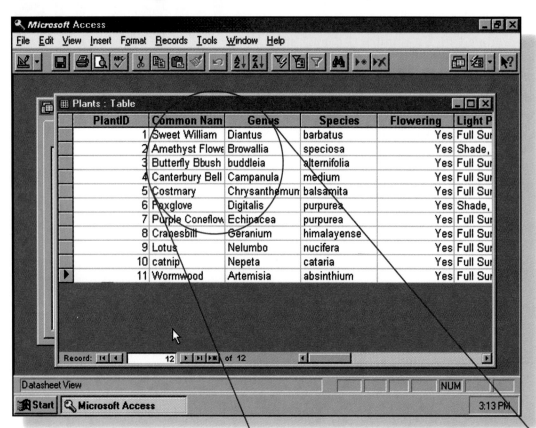

"Why would I do this?"

The reason for creating a database and the tables it contains is to store information in a format that you can use. Access stores your information as individual records in the various tables that you build. Each record consists of fields—single, logical divisions of information about the record. When you fill out a paper form you are completing a record. Each block that you complete is a specific field, whether it is a name, address, or date.

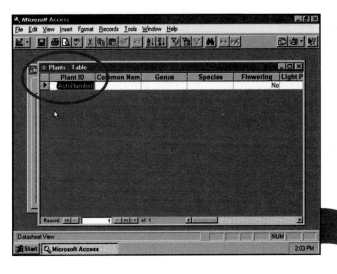

1 Start Access, open the **Garden Plants** database, and open the **Plants** table. You must open a table before you can begin to enter information into it.

2 Because there are no records in this table, only one record row displays. Press the **Tab** key to move the cursor from the Plant ID field to the Common Name field. Remember, the Plant ID field uses the AutoNumber data type. (Notice (AutoNumber) in the field.) Access doesn't permit you to enter any information into this field; it fills the field automatically.

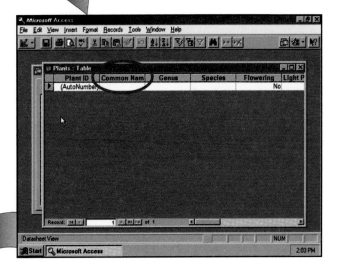

3 Type **Sweet William** into the Common Name field. Press the **Tab** key once again to move the cursor from the end of the text that you entered to the next field. Now that you have entered information into a field, Access assigns a number to the Plant ID field.

4 Type the following information into the remaining fields (you must press the **Tab** key after completing each entry): Genus: **Diantus**; Species: **barbatus**; Flowering: **Yes**; Light Preference: **Full Sun**; Fertilize Frequency: **Monthly**; Watering Frequency: **Keep Moist**; Date Purchased: **3/10/94**; Supplier: **St. John's Perennials**; Date Planted: **3/11/94**; Remarks: **Perennial**; FlowerColor: **Pink**; and NumberPlanted: **6**.

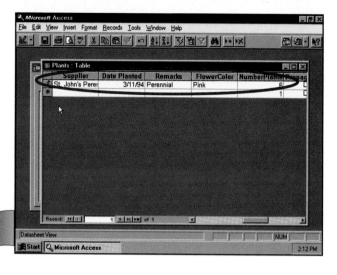

5 The final field in the table, PropagateBy-Seed, displays a small square box. This is the check box that you created when you added this field. You can propagate by seed, so either press the **Spacebar** on your keyboard, or click the check box. You see Access place a check mark in the box to indicate a "yes" response in this field.

NOTE ▼

You don't have to complete every field for every record. You can always add information to a record later.

6 Press the **Tab** key to complete the record. When you leave the record, Access automatically saves it. Complete the table using the information from the tables at the beginning of this part. Follow steps 1 through 6 for each record. ■

WHY WORRY?

If you make a mistake when entering information into a field, simply press Shift+Tab to move back to the field and retype the data.

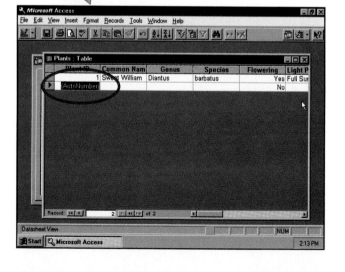

Copying Information from Another Record

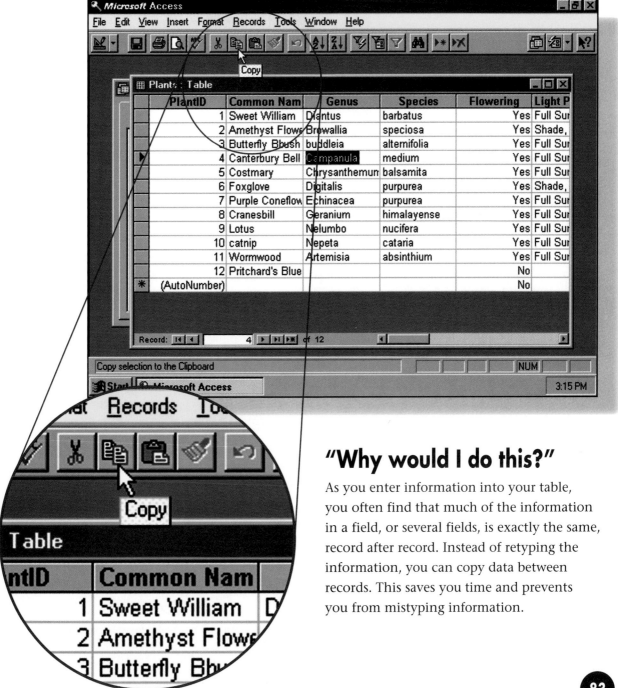

"Why would I do this?"

As you enter information into your table, you often find that much of the information in a field, or several fields, is exactly the same, record after record. Instead of retyping the information, you can copy data between records. This saves you time and prevents you from mistyping information.

1 Click the mouse pointer in the **Common Name** field in the blank record at the bottom of the table. Type **Pritchard's Blue** and press the **Tab** key to move to the next field.

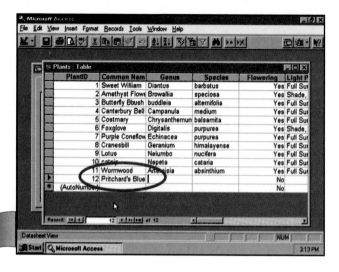

2 Move the mouse pointer up to the **Genus** field of plant 4, Canterbury Bell, and click once. You see the blinking insertion point in this cell. The insertion point's actual location within the cell depends upon where you position the mouse pointer when you click. Press the **Home** key to move the insertion point to the beginning of the word Campanula.

3 Press and hold the **Shift** key, and press the **End** key. This selects the entire entry in this cell. Let both keys go. Remember, when a cell and its contents appear on a black background with white text, it means the cell is selected.

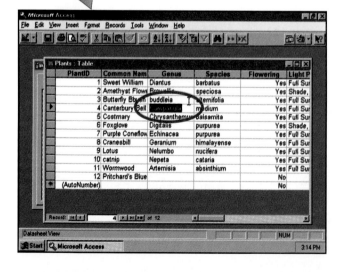

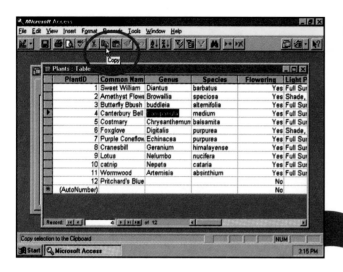

4 Click the **Copy** button from the toolbar. This copies the selected text to the Windows Clipboard. The text you copy remains on the Windows Clipboard until you either replace it with another selection or you exit from Windows.

NOTE ▼

You can also copy a selected cell to the Windows Clipboard with the Edit, Copy command.

5 Move the cursor back down to the **Genus** field for the new record at plant number 12. Click the **Paste** button on the toolbar. You see Access paste the text into the field.

NOTE ▼

If you want to copy information from the cell directly above the one the cursor is in, press the key combination Ctrl+' (Ctrl + single or double quote key). Access immediately copies and inserts the information in the cell directly above the current cell.

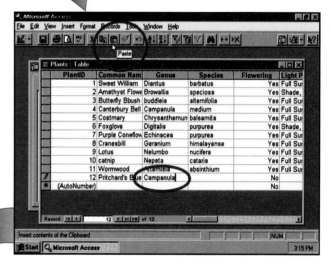

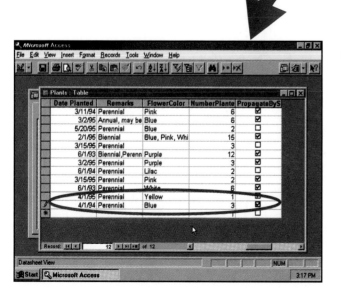

6 Type the remaining information into the indicated fields for this record: Species: **lactiflora**; Flowering: **Yes**; Light Preference: **Shade**; Fertilize Frequency: **Monthly**; Watering Frequency: **Keep moist**; Date Purchased: **4/1/94**; Supplier: **St. John's Perennials**; Date Planted: **4/1/94**; Remarks: **Perennial**; FlowerColor: **Blue**; NumberPlanted: **3**; and PropagateBySeed: check **Yes**. ■

Editing Data in a Field

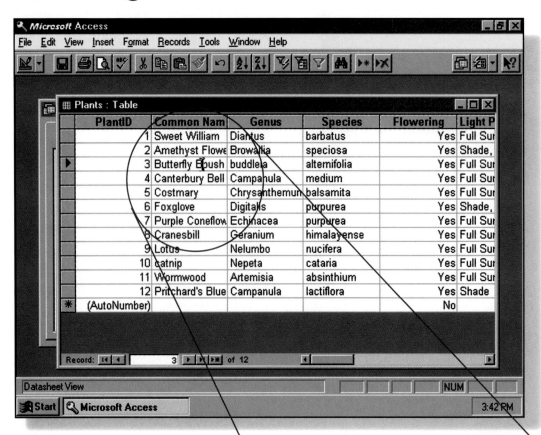

"Why would I do this?"

It is inevitable that you will need to edit some of your information at some time. You may find a misspelled entry in a field, or you may have to change a customer's address. You may even need to add information to a record that you did not have when you originally entered the data.

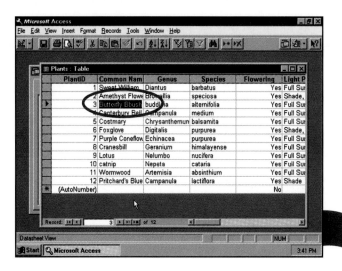

1 Move the cursor up to the Common Name field for record 3. The entry now reads Butterfly Bbush. Needless to say, the word "bush" does not have two "b's" in it.

2 Place the mouse pointer between the two "b's," in Bbush, and click once. You see the insertion point between these two letters. The cell text is not selected.

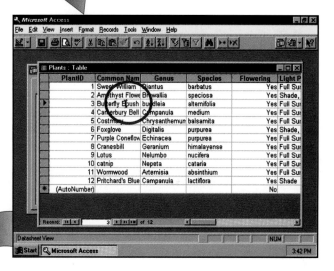

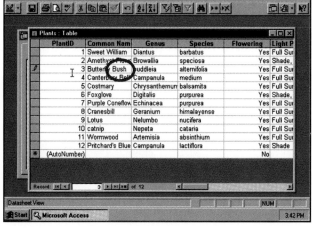

3 Press the **Delete** key once. This deletes the single "b" to the right of the insertion point.

NOTE ▼

Press the Backspace key to delete text to the left of the insertion point.

4 Press the **Tab** key once to move the insertion point to the **Genus** field, and press the **F2** key. The F2 key acts as a toggle button: with this key, you can switch between selecting all of the text in a cell and placing the insertion point at the end of the existing text.

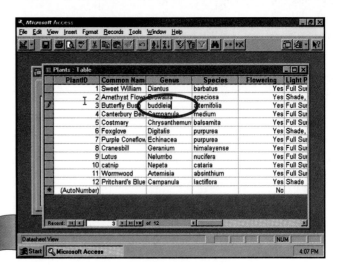

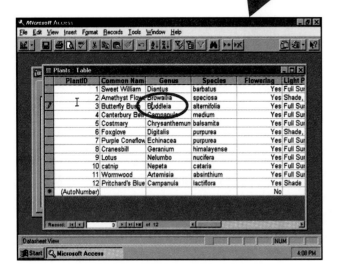

5 Press the **Home** key to move the insertion point to the beginning of the text in the cell, and press the **Delete** key to delete the letter "b." Now type **B** to complete this entry, making the entry's capitalization consistent with the rest of your records. ■

WHY WORRY?

You can edit any information that you have entered into a record at any time.

Undoing an Edit

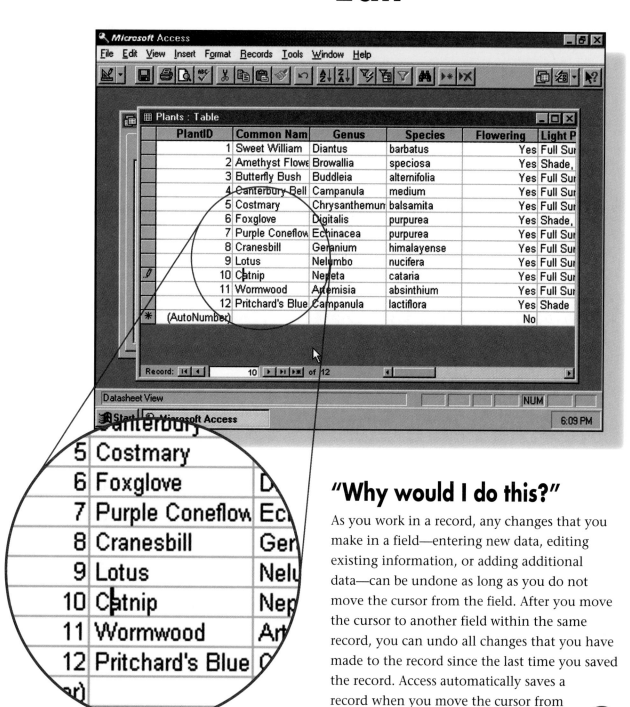

"Why would I do this?"

As you work in a record, any changes that you make in a field—entering new data, editing existing information, or adding additional data—can be undone as long as you do not move the cursor from the field. After you move the cursor to another field within the same record, you can undo all changes that you have made to the record since the last time you saved the record. Access automatically saves a record when you move the cursor from the record or close the table.

1 Move the cursor to record 10 in the **Common Name** field. This uncapitalized entry is not consistent with the others in this table. Type **Catnip**.

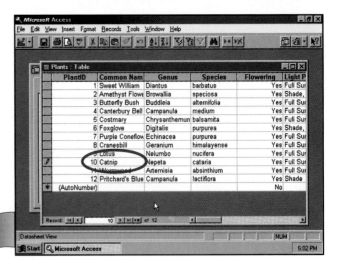

2 Click the **Undo** button on the toolbar. You see Access undo your editing, and the information returns to its unedited form.

> **NOTE** ▼
>
> You can also undo changes by selecting the Edit, Undo Current Field/Record command. You can also press the Esc key to do the same thing.

3 Type **Catnip** again. Press the **Tab** key to move to the next field in the same record and type **Nepetia**, another spelling of this genus that you believe you saw in a reference book.

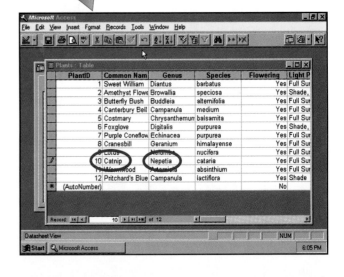

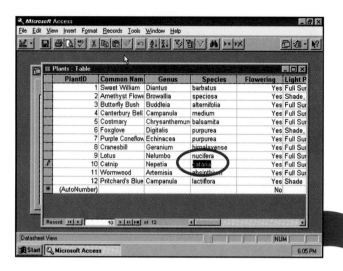

4 Press the **Tab** key to move to the next field. You now decide to check another one of your reference books to see what genus name it gives to the Catnip plant. Since it agrees with the first, you decide to change the information in the Genus field once again.

5 You can't simply undo your entry because you have already left the Genus field. Click the **Undo** button again. You now see Access reverse all of the changes you made in this record back to the original information. ■

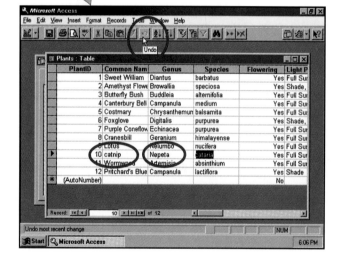

WHY WORRY?

Once you save a record by leaving it, you can still undo the changes by clicking the Undo button, selecting the Edit, Undo Saved Record command, or pressing Ctrl+Z. However, if you begin making changes to another record, you can't recover the original record.

Searching for Information

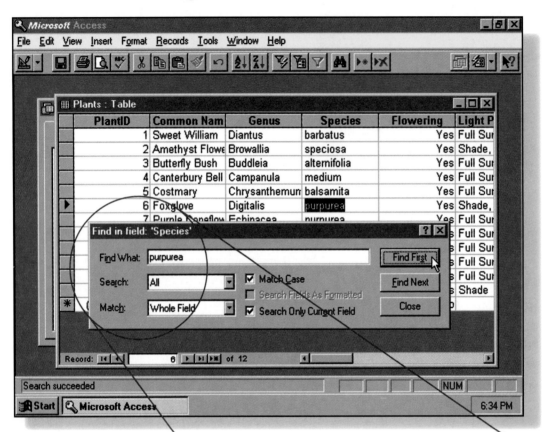

"Why would I do this?"

One of the greatest features of Access is its capability to find information quickly. How often have you tried to find information about a particular customer or product? Although Access keeps your records sorted by the key field set for the table, you can quickly search any field. In a table with many records it is much easier to use the Find command than to scroll through the records and risk missing the information that you are trying to find.

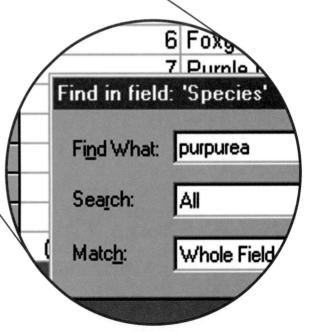

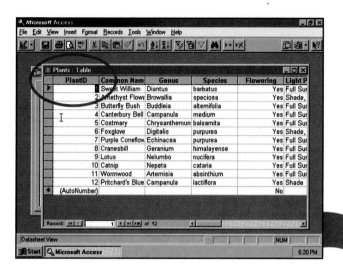

1 Open the **Plants** table if it is not already open. Access enables you to use the Find and Replace commands only in an open table or form.

> **NOTE** ▼
>
> You can also use the keyboard shortcut Ctrl+F, or the Edit, Find command to open the Find dialog box.

2 Click the mouse pointer in the **Species** field of the first record in the Plants table. This is the field you want Access to search through to find the information that you seek. Access can search through the entire table, but this can take several minutes if the table is large. Whenever possible, try to limit the search to the specific field in which you believe the information is.

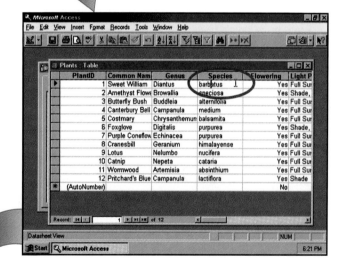

3 Click the **Find** button on the toolbar. You use the Find dialog box that appears to tell Access what you want to search for. As a reminder, Access displays the selected field in the dialog box title bar: **Find in field: 'Species'**.

4 Enter what you want Access to search for in the **Find What** text box. Type **purpurea** in the text box. When you do this, the Find First button becomes active.

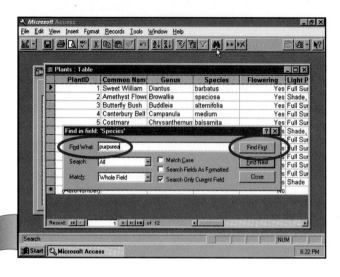

5 If you aren't sure of the location of the item you are looking for, select **All** from the **Search** combo box. You can also search **Up** the table from the cursor's current location (toward record number 1), or to search **Down** the table to the last record.

6 Use the **Match** combo box to choose how Access matches the text that you type in the Find What text box. Access searches all the fields specifically for what you enter using the default **Whole Field** option. Alternatively, you can select **Any Part of Field** to display a match if your text occurs anywhere in the field entry, or choose **Start of Field** to display an entry if your sample matches the beginning of any entry in the field.

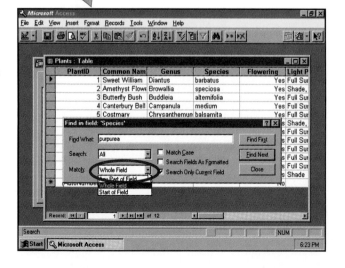

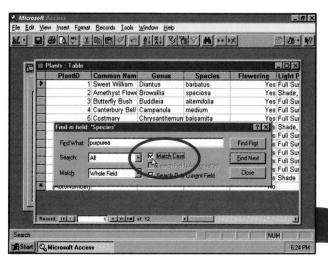

7 To find only those records that exactly match what you type in the Find What text box, click the **Match Case** check box. When you select this option, Access displays a record only if it exactly matches the upper- and lower-case letters you use. If you leave this option deselected, Access displays records such as: purpurea, Purpurea, or PURPUREA. With this option on, Access finds only the first example.

8 The **Search Only Current Field** option is selected by default. If you want to search the entire table, deselect this option. Deselecting this option increases the time that Access takes to search your table.

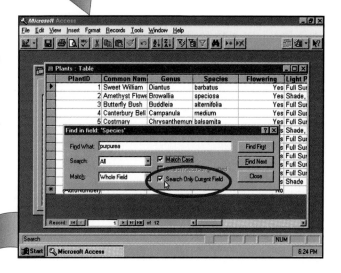

9 Click the **Find First** button to begin the search. After a few seconds, Access displays the first record it finds that meets the criteria you set in the Find dialog box.

95

10 Notice that Access moves the record selector indicator from record 1 to a new record. Click and drag the dialog box's title bar to move it down the screen until you can see this record. This record matches your search criteria.

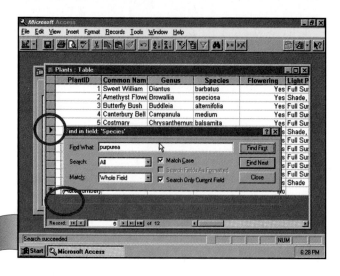

11 To search for any additional records that also meet the criteria, click the **Find Next** button. The record selector indicator moves down the table to the next record, and you can partially see a highlighted box behind the dialog box. Again, drag the dialog box so that you can see this record.

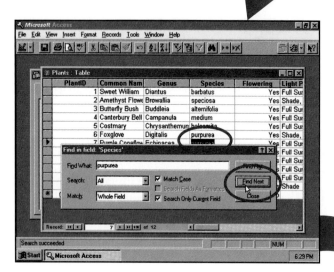

12 Click the **Find Next** button once again. You now see another dialog box telling you that Access found all the matching records. Click the **OK** button to close this dialog box and click the **Close** button to close the Find dialog box. ■

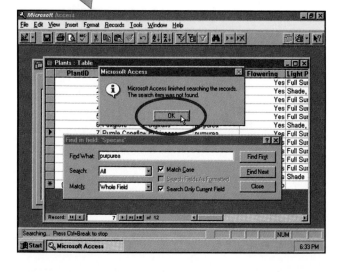

WHY WORRY?

If Access doesn't find what you type in the Find What text box, you can try some of the other settings in the Find dialog box. This enables Access to expand the search.

Replacing Selected Information

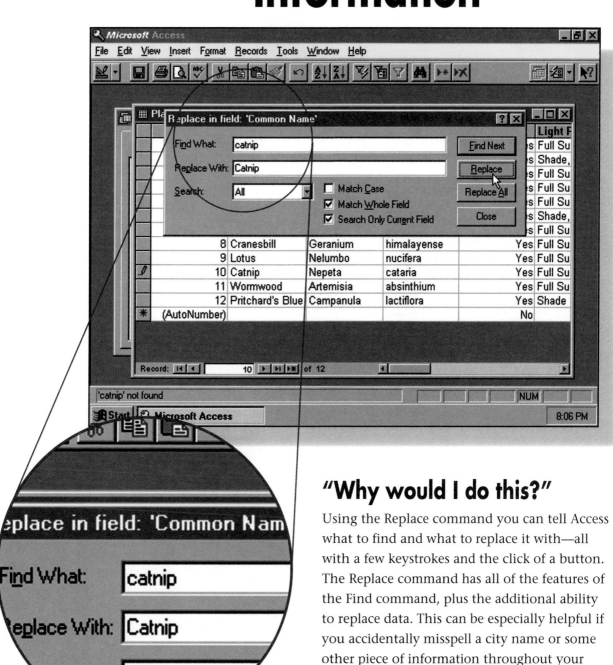

"Why would I do this?"

Using the Replace command you can tell Access what to find and what to replace it with—all with a few keystrokes and the click of a button. The Replace command has all of the features of the Find command, plus the additional ability to replace data. This can be especially helpful if you accidentally misspell a city name or some other piece of information throughout your table.

1 Click the mouse pointer in the **Common Name** field of the first record. Remember, you have not re-edited the entry for catnip from "catnip" to "Catnip" after undoing your changes on the record.

NOTE

Always be sure to start searches at the beginning of your table. You do this by placing the cursor in the first row of the field you want to search. Otherwise, Access begins the search with the record that the cursor is in.

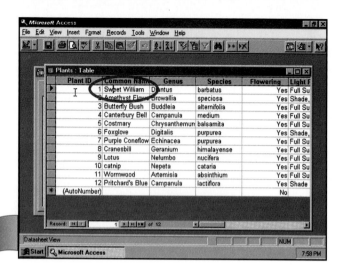

2 Select the **Replace** command from the **Edit** menu, or use the keyboard shortcut **Ctrl+H** to display the Replace dialog box. The dialog box title bar displays the field name Common Name, and the text you used in the Find dialog box now appears in the Replace dialog box. Access assumes that the last item it found is the item you want to replace.

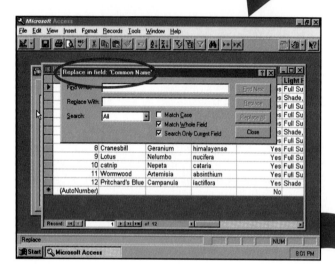

3 Type **catnip** into the **Find What** text box. When you enter text in this text box, Access overwrites any previous highlighted entry with the new entry.

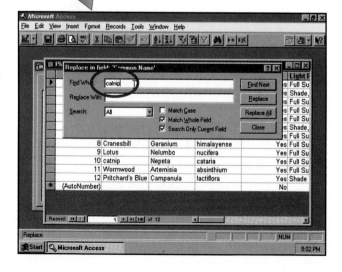

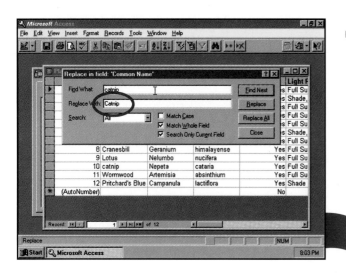

4 Press the **Tab** key to move to the **Replace With** text box. Type **Catnip** into this text box. Like the Find dialog box, you can use the options in the dialog box to tell Access where to search in the table and whether to search only for records that exactly match what you type.

5 Click the **Find Next** button. Access begins the search for the text you entered in the Find What text box. When Access finds a match, the record selector moves to that record and highlights the field, as you can see.

WHY WORRY?

If Access doesn't find any matches, you can try entering the find criteria in a slightly differently way, or deselect the Match Case or Match Whole Field options. These actions enable Access to expand the search.

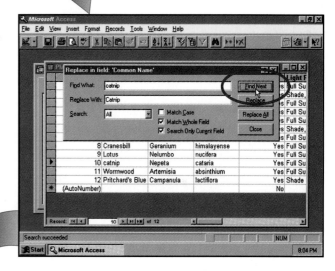

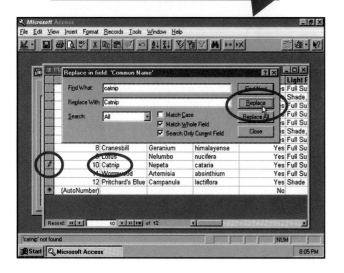

6 This is the field you want to replace, so click the **Replace** button. You see Access change the field's text to match the text in the Replace With text box. If you have another entry to search for, click the **Find Next** button again. The **Replace All** button enables Access to search for and replace all occurrences of the text throughout the table. Click the **Close** button to close the Replace dialog box. ■

Sorting Records

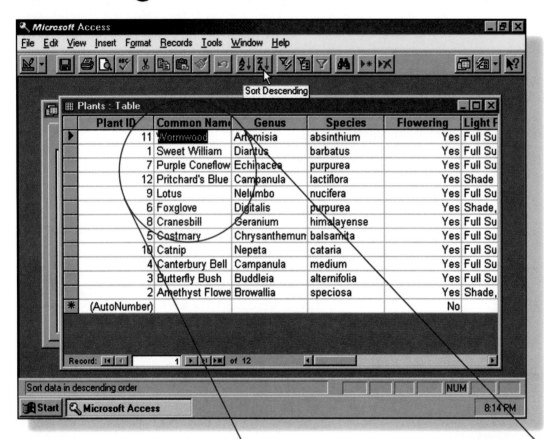

"Why would I do this?"

Most tables use a key field to create a unique record identifying field with the AutoNumber data type. Access automatically sorts all of the tables records with this field, from the smallest to largest record number. The records Access sorts in this manner aren't often the easiest to scroll through when you want to view groups of records. For example, if you want to view the plants listed in your table, you probably want to see them in alphabetical order, not numerical order.

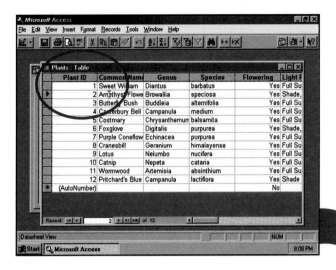

1 Open the **Plants** table if it is not already open on your screen. Move the cursor to the **Common Name** field by clicking the mouse pointer in column. It does not matter if you move the cursor to the first record or to some other record.

> **NOTE** ▼
>
> Remember, you can move from one field to the next by pressing either the Tab key or the arrow keys.

2 Click the right mouse button to display a shortcut menu.

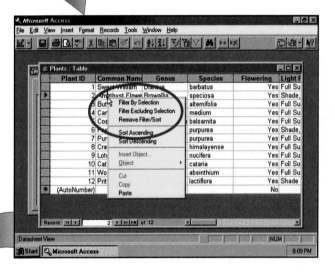

3 Select the **Sort Ascending** option from the shortcut menu. If all of your data in the field begins with letters, the ascending sort order is an alphabetical sort order. An ascending sort order that includes numbers looks like this: 1, 2, 3, a, B, c, D,...y, Z. The sort order is not case-sensitive for text.

4 Click the **Sort Descending** button on the toolbar. You now see Access re-sort the list in a descending order by Common Name.

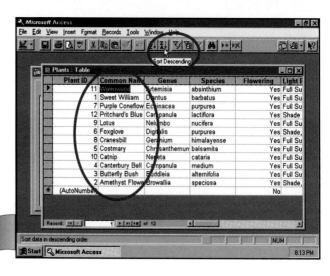

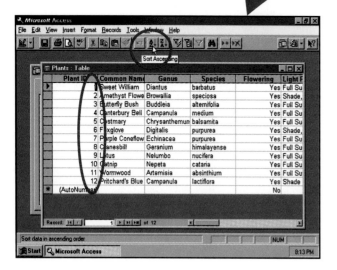

5 Move the cursor to the **Plant ID** column and click the **Sort Ascending** button to resort the table in its original order. ∎

WHY WORRY?

Once you close a table that uses a key field, such as the Plant ID field, Access automatically re-sorts the table according to this key field the next time you use the table.

Deleting a Selected Record

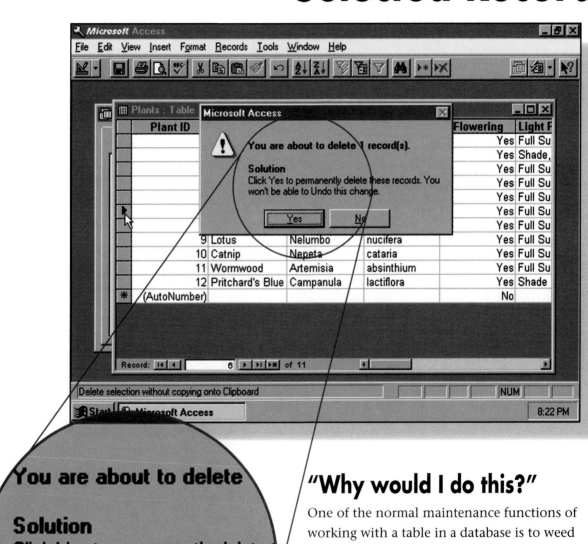

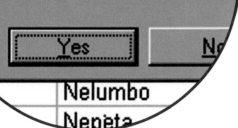

"Why would I do this?"

One of the normal maintenance functions of working with a table in a database is to weed out old, unnecessary information from the table. As you add new records to a table, you eventually find that you no longer use some records. For example, there may be records for a customer who no longer buys from you, a discontinued inventory item, or, in the case of the Plants table, a certain plant you no longer grow. When this occurs, you may want to delete these records from the table.

103

1 Move the mouse pointer to the record selector box for plant number 6, Foxglove. Notice how the mouse pointer changes shape to a right-facing arrow.

NOTE ▼

You can easily deselect a record by clicking the mouse pointer on any field.

2 Click the left mouse button once. You see Access select the entire record.

NOTE ▼

You can also use the Edit, Cut command, or the Cut button on the toolbar to delete a record. When you cut a record, Access places a copy of it on the Windows Clipboard, enabling you to recover the record later from the Clipboard if necessary.

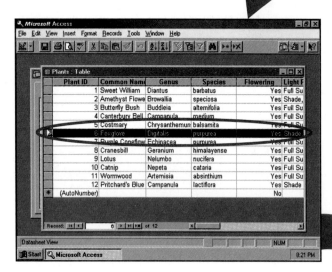

3 Press the **Delete** key on your keyboard, and Access deletes the record. A confirmation dialog box displays on-screen telling you how many records will be deleted. Click the **Yes** button to confirm that you want to delete a record, or **No** if you want to restore the record. ■

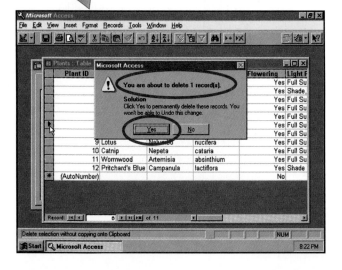

Moving a Field Column

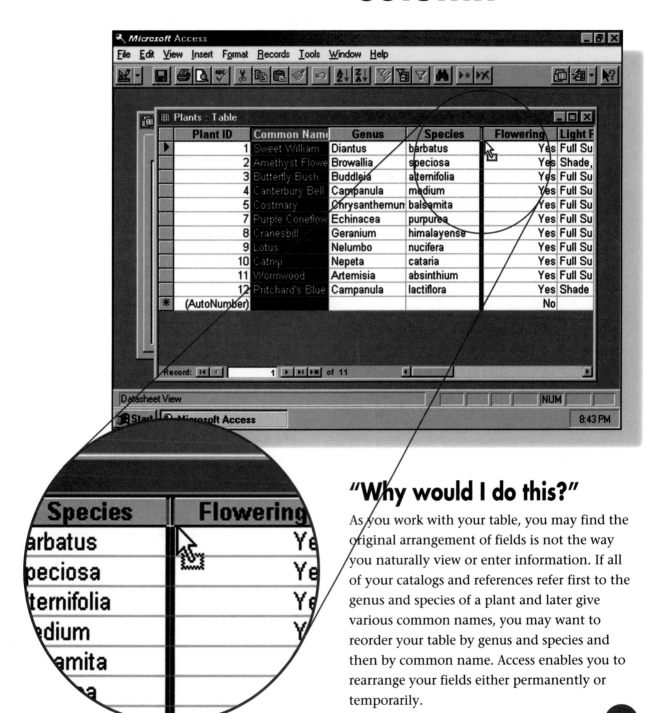

"Why would I do this?"

As you work with your table, you may find the original arrangement of fields is not the way you naturally view or enter information. If all of your catalogs and references refer first to the genus and species of a plant and later give various common names, you may want to reorder your table by genus and species and then by common name. Access enables you to rearrange your fields either permanently or temporarily.

1 Open the **Plants** table if it is not already open. Move the mouse pointer to the column label **Common Name** and click the left mouse button once. The mouse is in the right position when it changes shape to a downward facing arrow.

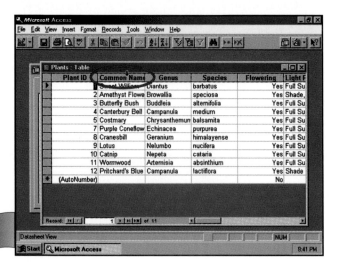

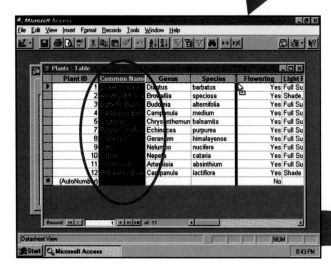

2 Click to select the column and drag the column to its new location. You see a heavy, thick column bar between fields as you move the mouse pointer indicating places where you can drop the field. Move the mouse pointer until the heavy line is between the Species and Flowering columns.

WHY WORRY?

If you do not quite get the column where you want, simply drag it again.

3 Let go of the mouse button and drop the field in its new location. Save this new table configuration by clicking the **Save** button on the toolbar.

NOTE ▼

If you only want to change the table configuration while you are working on it during an editing session, don't click on the Save button.

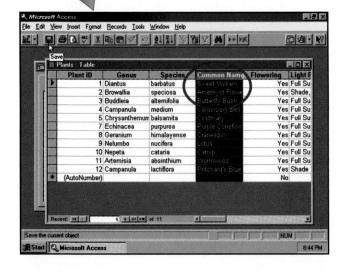

Resizing Rows or Columns

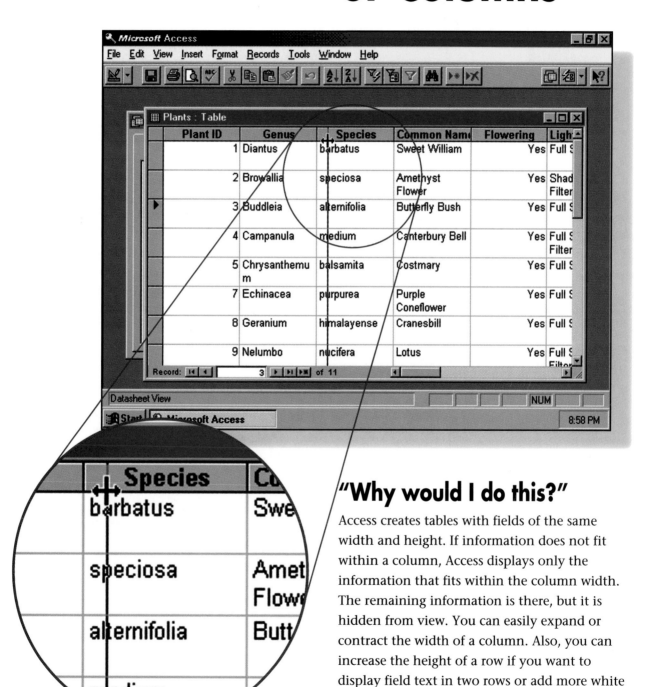

"Why would I do this?"

Access creates tables with fields of the same width and height. If information does not fit within a column, Access displays only the information that fits within the column width. The remaining information is there, but it is hidden from view. You can easily expand or contract the width of a column. Also, you can increase the height of a row if you want to display field text in two rows or add more white space between records.

1 You can easily change the height of your rows by moving the mouse pointer to any point between two Row Selection buttons. You see the mouse pointer change shape to resemble a horizontal line with up- and down-arrow facing arrows.

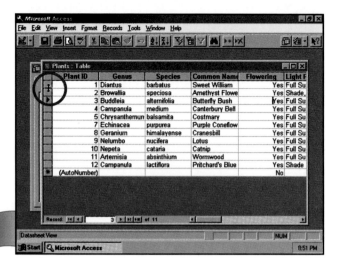

> **NOTE** ▼
>
> Access doesn't automatically adjust the size of the font you use when you decrease the height of your records. If you decrease the height too much, your records appear to overlap each other, and you may see only the top half of each letter.

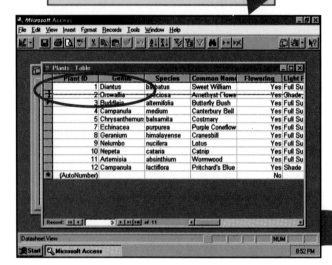

2 Press the left mouse button and drag the mouse pointer down. This increases the row height. Notice the dark line extending from the mouse pointer across the table. This line indicates the new width of your row. You can decrease the row's width by moving the pointer up.

3 Release the mouse button. You now see the new row height set to the size you want. By increasing the row height, you add additional white space to the records, giving the table a less cramped appearance. The changes you make to the row height affect all records in the table.

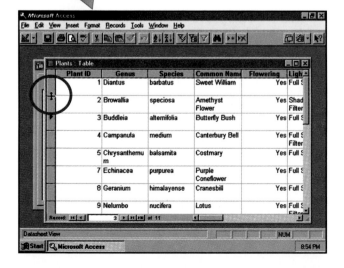

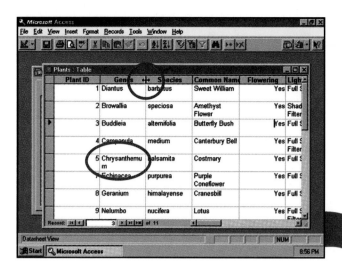

4 Notice that the entry **Chrysanthemum** in the Genus field dropped its final "m" to the second line in the field. Move the mouse pointer to the dividing line between the **Genus** and **Species** field labels. The mouse pointer again changes shape—to a vertical line with a left- and right-facing arrow.

NOTE ▼

Always select the dividing line to the right of the column with the width you want to adjust.

5 Press the left mouse button and drag the column to the right, increasing the width of the column. You see a solid line extend from the mouse pointer to the bottom of the table to indicate the new column width.

WHY WORRY?

You can increase or decrease the width of a field, or the height of a record at any time. The size of a field or record does not affect the information that the field or record contains.

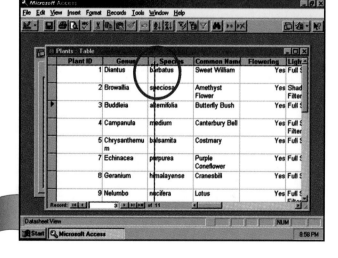

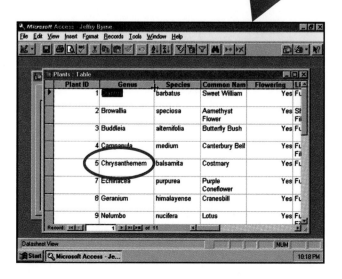

6 Release the mouse button to set the new field size. Notice how Access automatically adjusts the text in the column by moving the letter "m" back up with the rest of the word. Close the table by clicking the **Close** button. Be sure not to save the revised table layout. The adjustments you make to the field width affect only the selected columns. ■

Freezing and Unfreezing Columns

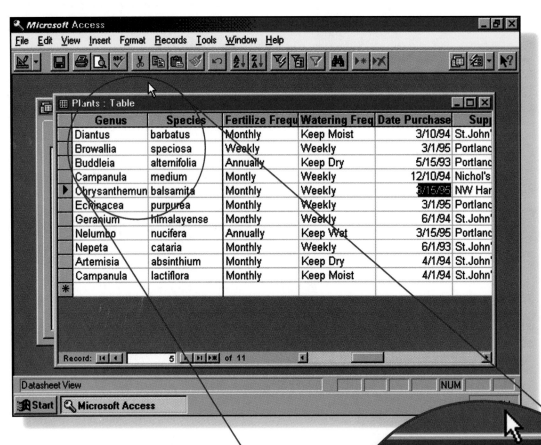

"Why would I do this?"

When you view or enter information into a table that stretches across many fields and several screen widths, the first few fields that you identify each record by usually scroll away from view. You can easily freeze a column so it remains in the leftmost position in the table. As you scroll through your table, this reference field always remains visible.

1 Open the **Plants** table if it is not already open. Move the mouse pointer to the **Genus** column label and click it once to select the column. Remember, the mouse pointer changes to a downward facing arrow when it is in the correct position for you to select the column.

2 Press the key combination **Shift+right arrow** key to select the **Species** column. You don't have to select the current left-most column as one of those to freeze in place; you can choose any adjacent fields that make sense to you.

NOTE ▼

You also can choose multiple columns by selecting the first column you want to freeze and drag the mouse pointer across the other adjacent columns until you select all the columns you want.

3 Open **Format** menu and select **Freeze Columns**. You see Access shift the selected columns to the left-most position in the table.

4 Press the **Tab** key, or use the horizontal scroll bar at the bottom of the table window, to scroll through your table. Notice that Access displays a solid black line between the frozen columns and the unfrozen columns. As you scroll through the fields, you see the frozen columns remain in place while the unfrozen columns scroll across the window.

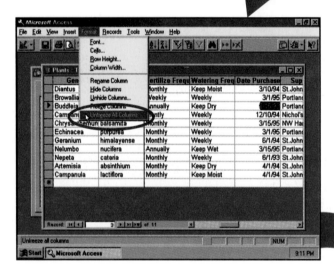

5 Open the **Format** menu bar and select **Unfreeze All Columns**. Access removes the solid dividing line and restores the table to normal scrolling—all columns moving—but doesn't shift the columns to their original positions.

WHY WORRY?

If you reposition the columns, Access asks you if you want to save this new table format. Select the No button to return the columns to their original positions; or select the Yes button if you want to make this new table format permanent.

6 Click the column label **Genus** and drag the mouse pointer across the screen to the **Species** column to select these fields. Now, drag these fields back to their original position between the **Plant ID** and **Common Name** fields. ■

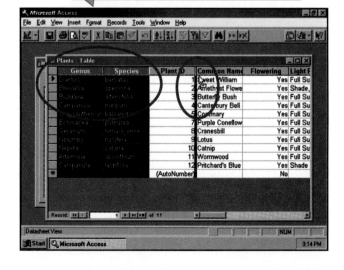

Hiding and Unhiding Columns

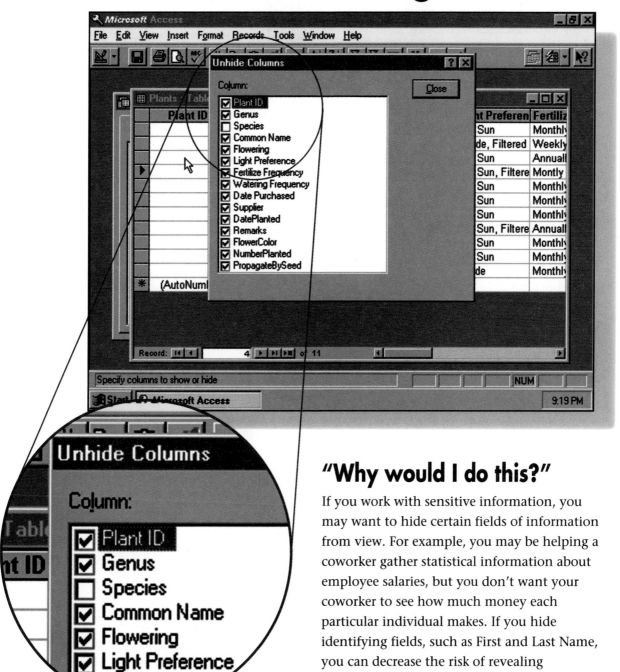

"Why would I do this?"

If you work with sensitive information, you may want to hide certain fields of information from view. For example, you may be helping a coworker gather statistical information about employee salaries, but you don't want your coworker to see how much money each particular individual makes. If you hide identifying fields, such as First and Last Name, you can decrease the risk of revealing confidential information.

1 Open the **Plants** table if necessary. Move the cursor to any record in the column you want to hide, such as the **Species** column. Open the **Format** menu bar and select **Hide Columns**.

NOTE ▼

When you need to quickly hide a single column, select it and then click the right mouse button to display a shortcut menu with a Hide Columns option.

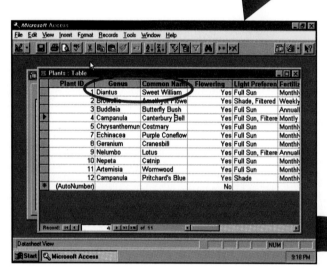

2 Access hides the column with the cursor located within it from view.

NOTE ▼

You can hide multiple adjacent columns by first selecting them and then choosing Format, Hide Columns from the menu.

3 To unhide columns, open the **Format** menu and choose **Unhide Columns**. You see the Unhide Columns dialog box appear on-screen.

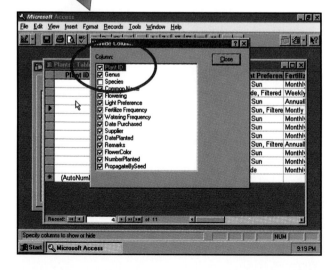

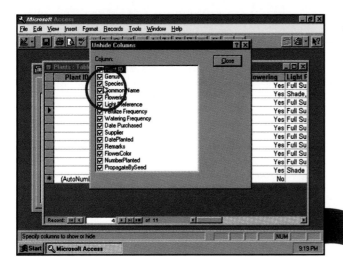

4 Notice that only one field name's check box is unchecked, the hidden column Species. Click in the check box. You see your table blink behind the dialog box as Access unhides the Species column.

NOTE ▼

Remember, you can use the arrow keys to move through the options in a dialog box. Also, you can press the Spacebar to check and uncheck a check box option.

5 Click the **Close** button to return to the table. You see the **Species** column in the table in its regular position. ■

NOTE ▼

You can also use the Unhide Columns dialog box to hide columns that aren't adjacent to each other. Simply click in the corresponding check boxes to remove the check mark from all columns that you want to hide. Access hides all columns that don't have a check mark.

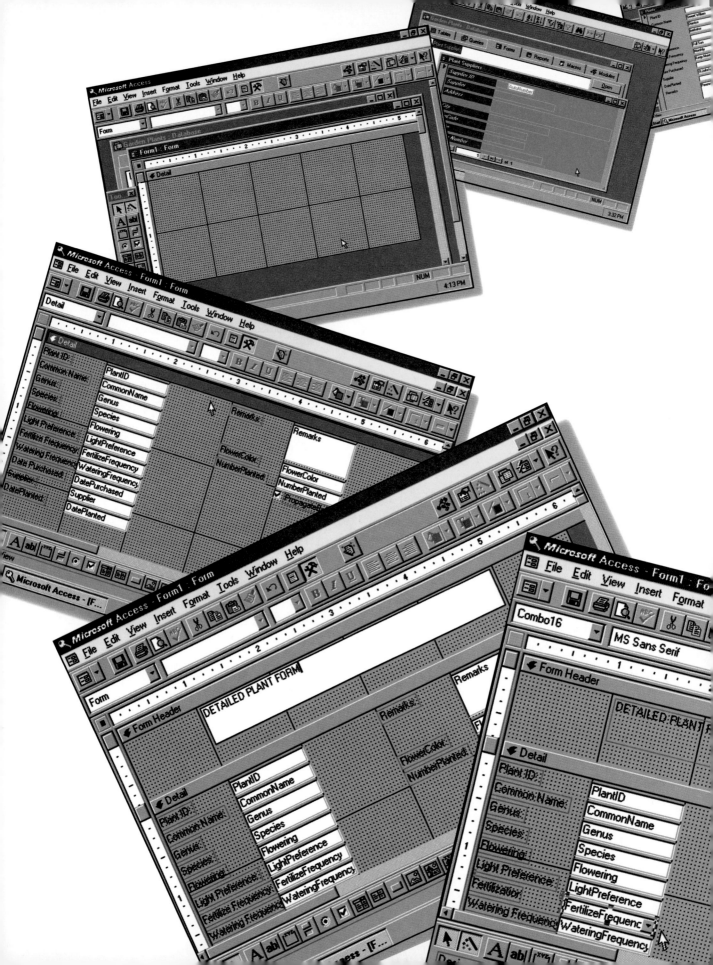

PART IV

Using Database Forms

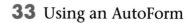

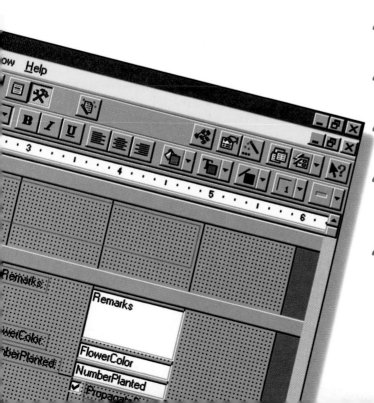

Now that you are familiar with using a table to view, enter, edit, and delete information with Access, it's time to learn how to create and use a form. An Access form displays information in a variety of formats. You can view and edit groups of records, or display all of the fields of a single record within a form.

A form is often a simple on-screen representation of a paper form. You can design the form to present each record on its own form or page. If you need to see more than a single record at a time, you can easily switch back to the table, or datasheet, mode with the click of a button.

You can use one of three basic tools to build a form: the Form Wizard, Design View, or an AutoForm. The Form Wizard helps you to build a form by leading you through a series of question and answer dialog boxes. With Design View you can create your form totally from scratch, or edit a form you created with the Form Wizard or an AutoForm. An AutoForm is a pre-designed form. You simply choose from three AutoForms and then tell Access where to find the information (records) to input into the AutoForm. You will probably find that working with the Form Wizard is the best way to get your feet wet, rather than designing a form from a blank window.

You can choose from among several formats for the labels and fields of your form, including:

Style	How It Looks on Your Form
Clouds	This form has a cloud and sky background. Fields appear in a light gray box, with labels shown to the left. Text in fields and labels appears in a similar font in black.
Colorful 1	The background for the form is a solid color. Fields appear in a contrasting color box, and labels appear with a different color background to the left. Text in fields and labels appear in white, and the text for labels is a bold, italic font.
Colorful 2	This form uses a background that is a solid color, though lighter than Colorful 1. Fields appear in an embossed box, with labels on the left. Black text appears in fields; red, bold text appears in labels.
Dusk	This background is a dark twilight blue with a cityscape at the bottom and stars at the top. Fields appear in a box with white text; labels contain bold text in yellow, on the left.

Style	How It Looks on Your Form
Evergreen	This background is a medium green. Fields are displayed with green text in an embedded box. The labels are in black, bold text on the left.
Flax	The background of this form is a flaxen color with a diagonal strip. Fields appear in a raised, shadowed box with black text. Labels, on the left, are a bold, white text.
International	A stylized flat globe appears on this form's background. Fields appear in raised, shadowed boxes with black text. Labels, on the left, are displayed in blue, bold text.
Pattern	This form uses a green background with a mottled, square pattern. Fields are displayed in a gray box with a dashed line border, and black text. Labels are on the left in a bold, white font.
Standard	This form, similar to a standard Win95 dialog box, has a gray background. Fields appear in an embedded box with a white background and black text. Labels are on the left, in black.
Stone	This form displays a background with a mottled gray and white pattern that appears like stone. Fields are shown in a gray box with black text. Labels are displayed with a red, bold font in an embossed box.

You have three AutoForm formats that you can select, each of which automatically displays all fields from the selected table:

AutoForm	Looks Like
Columnar	This form displays all fields in a column with their labels on the left. Multiple columns will be created when necessary for a table containing many fields.
Tabular	Each record appears in a single row and scrolls across the form. Labels appear once at the top of the form.
Datasheet	This AutoForm appears like a normal datasheet with records in rows and labels at the top. All fields appear at the width specified in the tables Field Size property.
AutoForm button on toolbar	The background is light gray. Fields and labels are in a single column. Fields appear in white, sunken boxes with black text. Field labels are on the left side in black text.

Using an AutoForm

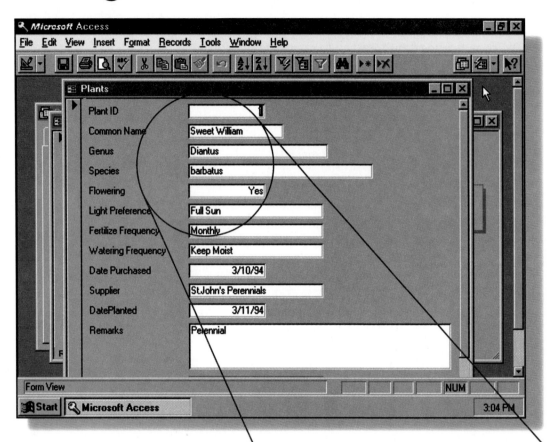

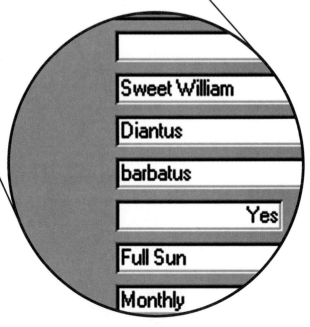

"Why would I do this?"

To quickly view all fields for each record in a selected table without scrolling back and forth across the table, you can use an AutoForm. Each Access AutoForm creates a simple table based upon a selected table. You don't have any control over how fields appear.

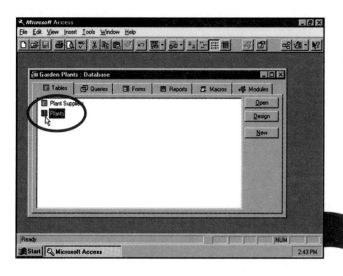

1 Open the **Garden Plants** database and select the **Plants** table. You don't have to actually open the table, you simply need to select it by clicking it once with the mouse pointer.

WHY WORRY?

If you do open the Plants table, just continue on to the next step. The AutoForm works just as well from an open table as it does with a selected table.

2 Move the mouse pointer to the down arrow on the **New Object** button on the toolbar and click it once. The New Object button actually has two parts. The down arrow part displays a list of several new object types that you can build, while the icon part on the left half of the button shows the currently selected new object. You can immediately launch the currently selected new object by clicking the icon.

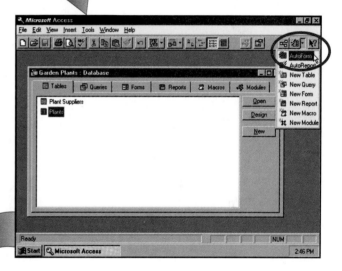

3 Choose **AutoForm** from the drop-down list. After a few seconds you see the AutoForm for the Plants table appear on your screen. Use the scroll bars on the right and bottom of the form window to view the rest of the form. Click the **Close** button and do not save the form. ■

Building a Form with a Wizard

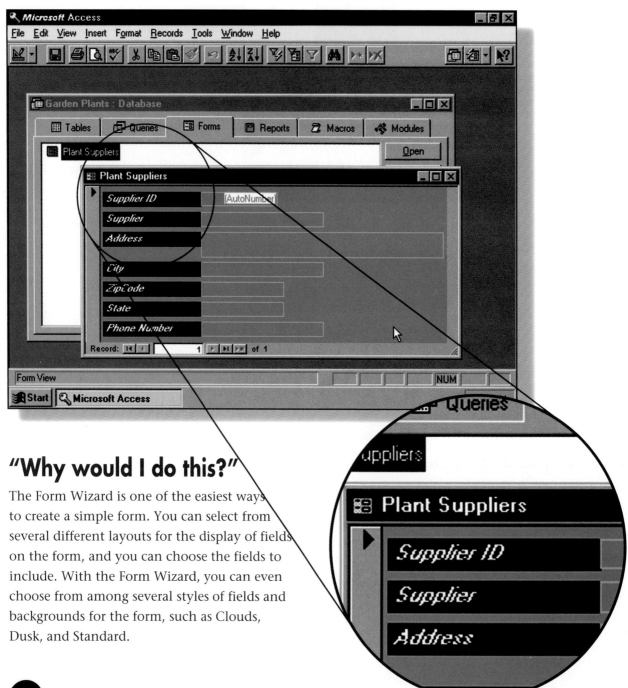

"Why would I do this?"

The Form Wizard is one of the easiest ways to create a simple form. You can select from several different layouts for the display of fields on the form, and you can choose the fields to include. With the Form Wizard, you can even choose from among several styles of fields and backgrounds for the form, such as Clouds, Dusk, and Standard.

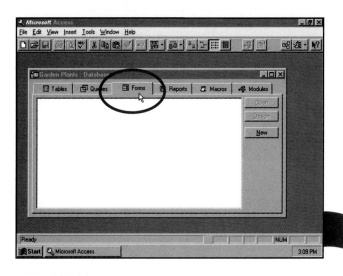

1 Use the mouse pointer to click the **Forms** button on the database window. Just like the Tables list, any forms that you create and save appear here. This list is empty because you have not saved any forms yet.

2 Click the **New** button, or press **Ctrl+N**. The New Form dialog box appears.

NOTE ▼

You can also select the Form command from the Insert menu to open the New Form dialog box.

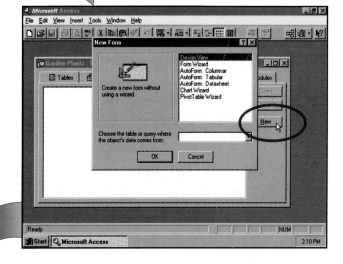

3 In the top list box, select the **Form Wizard** option. In the combo box below the list, click the arrow to display the list of objects on which you can base this form. Choose the **Plant Suppliers**, and then click the **OK** button.

4 You now see the first of several Form Wizard dialog boxes. In the Available Field list box you choose the fields to include in your new form. Select the field you want to insert in the form and click the > button to move the field from the Available Fields list box to the Selected Fields list box.

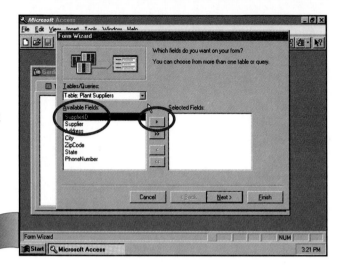

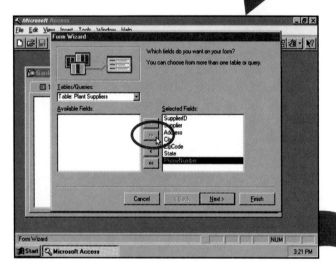

5 You want to include the fields from the Plant Suppliers table in the new form, so click the **>>** button to move all of the fields. You see the fields move from the Available Fields list box to the Selected Fields list box.

WHY WORRY?

If you decide not to include a field, select it from the Selected Fields list box and click the < button to remove it. The field appears in the Available Fields list box again. To deselect all of the fields and start over, click the << button.

6 Click the **Next>** button to move to the next dialog box. You must now choose from three layout options. Click each option button to preview approximately how your table will appear in each layout. Choose the option button **Columnar**.

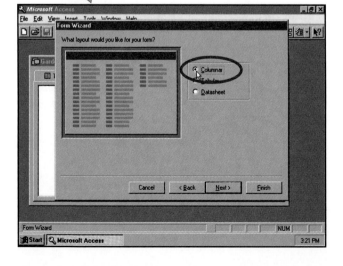

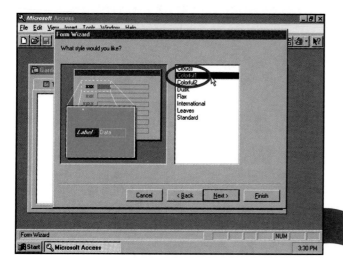

7 Click the **Next>** button. This dialog box enables you to select from eight background and field/label combination styles. Select the **Colorful1** option from the list.

NOTE ▼

If you are not sure of a choice you made in a previous dialog box, click the Back button to move back to it. You can then make any adjustments and then step through the dialog boxes by using the Next buttons again.

8 Click the **Next>** button. In this dialog box you choose a title for the form. Access enters a default title which is the same as the object on which the form is based. If you don't like the title, just type what you want. Click the **Finish** button, and Access completes your form and displays it.

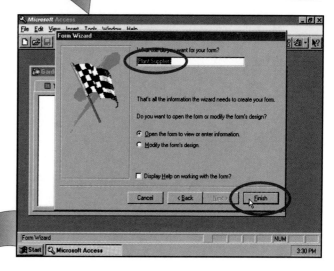

9 Close the form by clicking the **Close** button in the corner of the window. You see the form's name in the Forms list on the database window. Access automatically saves your new form for you. ■

WHY WORRY?

If your new form doesn't work the way you want, you can always revise it. Or, if you don't use the form, delete it.

Opening the Form Design View Window

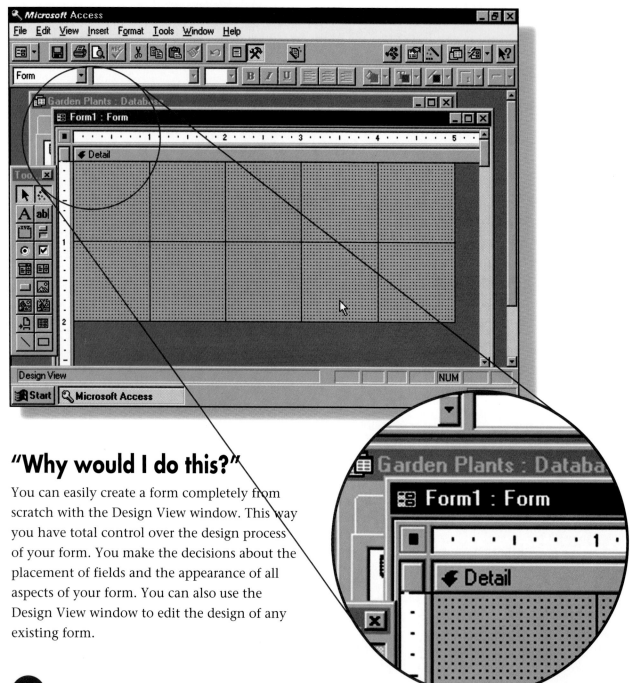

"Why would I do this?"

You can easily create a form completely from scratch with the Design View window. This way you have total control over the design process of your form. You make the decisions about the placement of fields and the appearance of all aspects of your form. You can also use the Design View window to edit the design of any existing form.

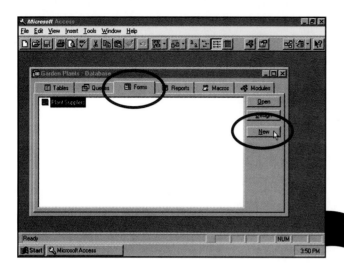

1 From the Database window click the **Forms** tab, displaying the Forms list. This list shows the Plant Suppliers form that you created. Click the **New** button.

2 The New Form dialog box appears. In the upper list box, select the **Design View** option. In the combo box below, choose the **Plants** table as the base for the form. Click the **OK** button.

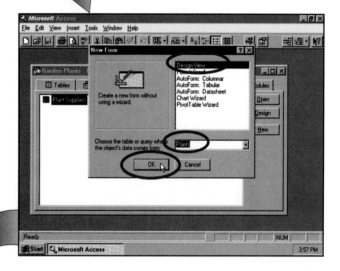

3 You now see the Design View window on your screen. From this window you can build your own unique form, which is explained in the following tasks. ■

NOTE ▼

Access replaces the Standard toolbar with two new toolbars—Form Design and Formatting—and a floating toolbox—called the Toolbox. You use these tools to build forms.

127

Adding Fields to a Form

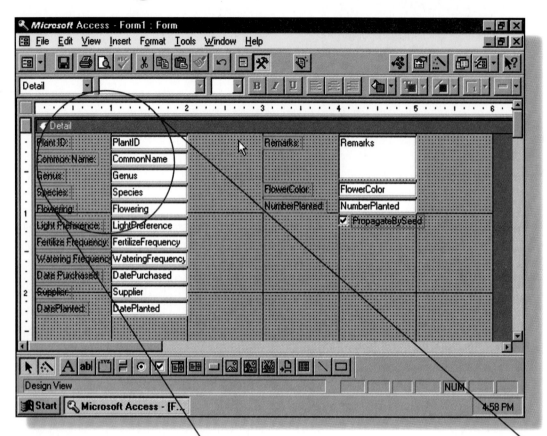

"Why would I do this?"

The basic purpose of using a form is for you to be able to view, enter, and edit information both quickly and easily. Access then adds this information to the table without you having to directly input it. Before you can begin to add information into your form, you must add fields from the table to the blank form.

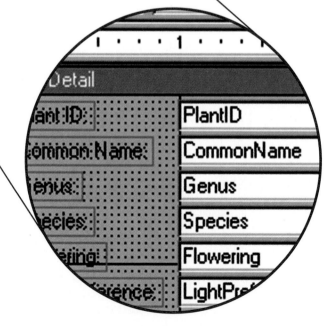

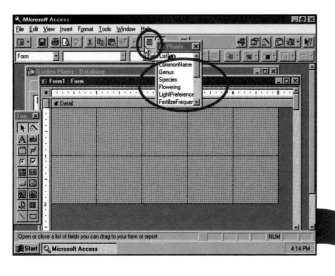

1 Use the mouse pointer and click the **Field List** button. You see a floating list box showing the available fields that you can use in your form.

NOTE ▼

When you place a field on the blank form, you see that two boxes with the same name in them appear on the form. The box on the right is the actual field, while the one on the left is the field's label. When you complete your form, the label box still shows the label for the field, while the field box remains blank until you enter information into it.

2 Click on and drag the **Plant ID** field from the floating list box to the Detail area of the form. You see the mouse pointer arrow change shape to a representation of a field.

NOTE ▼

If you have a lot of fields to place in the form but not very much room in the detail area, click the Maximize button on the form window to increase the detail area. The figures in this task have been Maximized.

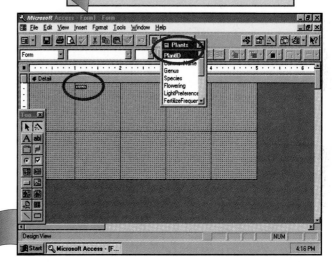

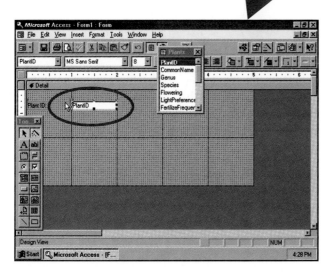

3 Move the mouse pointer to the location below the Detail bar and beside the black one-inch line on the horizontal ruler and drop the field by releasing the mouse button.

NOTE ▼

You can quickly remove the floating list box by clicking the Close button on it, or clicking the Field List button again.

4 You can move a field and its label by moving the mouse pointer to an edge of the field. You see the pointer change shape to resemble a hand. Click and drag the field and label to a new position. As you drag the field, an outline of the field and label text boxes move with you so that you can place them accurately.

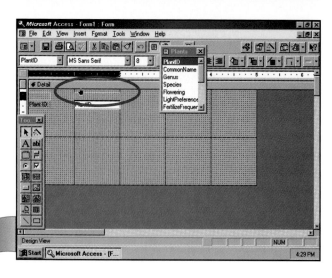

NOTE ▼

The eight black squares that surround the field box are handles. Use the largest handle in the upper-left corner to move the box; the other seven change the size of the box.

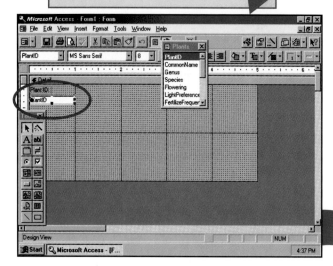

5 You can move the label and field independently of each other. Move the mouse pointer to the large handle in the upper-left corner of the field box and drag it to its new position. Move the field and label boxes back to their original positions.

NOTE ▼

You may want to move a field and its label independently from each other if for example you want to display the labels above their fields. When the mouse pointer changes to a hand with a pointing finger, you have placed it on the correct handle.

6 Select and drag the field **CommonName** from the field list to the Detail form area, beneath the Plant ID field. Do the same for the fields **Genus** and **Species**.

NOTE ▼

Use the horizontal and vertical rulers to estimate the size of the form's Detail area and the placement and size of the objects.

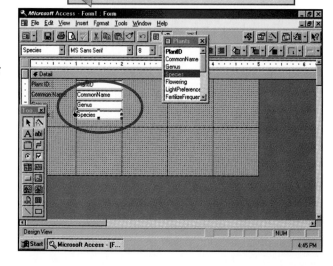

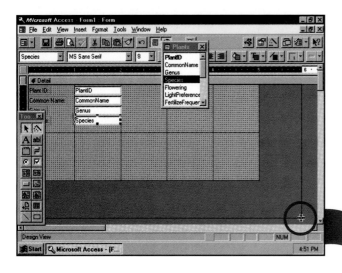

7 To make more room, move the mouse pointer to the lower-right corner of the Detail area. You again see the mouse pointer change shape, this time to a four-headed arrow. Click and drag the corner down and to the right until it is approximately six inches long by three inches in width.

8 Drag the remaining fields to the Detail area. Click the **Close** button on the floating list box when you finish adding fields. ■

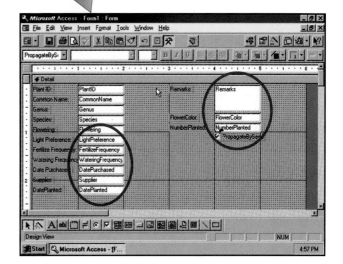

WHY WORRY?

If you can't see the vertical ruler, simply move the toolbox to a new location by clicking and dragging its title bar. Dragging it to one of the edges of your screen causes it to adhere itself to the edge like a toolbar. You can change it or any toolbar to a floating toolbox by dragging it away from the screen edge.

NOTE ▼

As you place each field, notice how neatly the fields align to the lines or rows of dots in the Detail area. The rows of dots and lines act like magnets to attract your fields to the closest part of the grid. This feature is called *Snap to Grid*; it helps you adjust and align all of the objects that you place on your form.

Creating Labels

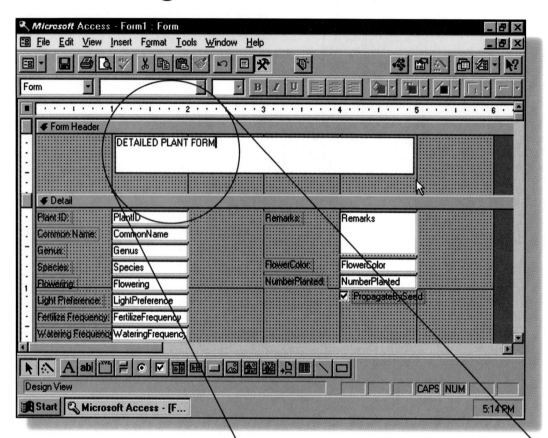

"Why would I do this?"

You can create your own labels to give your form a more professional appearance and make it easier to use. By adding text for titles or other information, you can help increase the usability of your form. For example, if you aren't the only person who is using this form, you can add a small label box of instructions about how to use the form and enter information to get other users off to a good start.

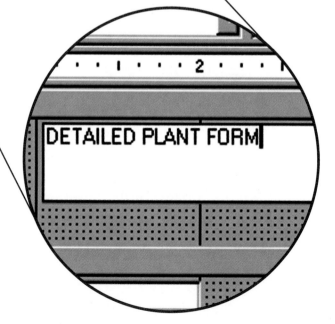

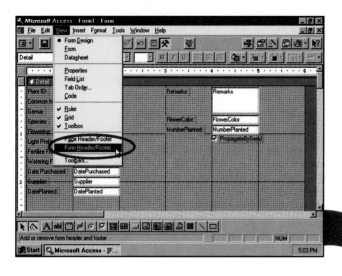

1 Open the **View** menu and choose the **Form Header/Footer** command, to place both a form header and footer area. You now see a new blank area above the Detail bar. This is the Form Header area. If you use the vertical scroll bar, you can see the corresponding Form Footer area at the bottom of your form.

2 Move the mouse pointer to the top edge of the Detail bar. You see the pointer change shape to a solid horizontal bar with arrows pointing up and down. Drag the edge of the Form Header down about $^1/_2$-inch, increasing the width of the Form Header to about $^3/_4$-inch.

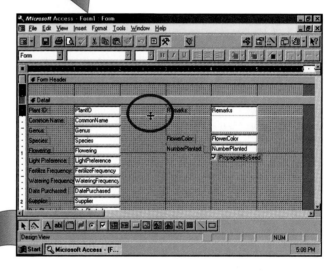

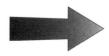

3 From the toolbox, select the **Label** button. Move the mouse pointer (now in the shape of the letter "A" with a plus sign) up to the Form Header. Position the crosshairs, or plus sign, at the location where you want the upper-left corner of your label to begin.

4 Drag diagonally across to the opposite corner where you want the label box to end and release the mouse button. A blank label box now appears with a blinking insertion point inside.

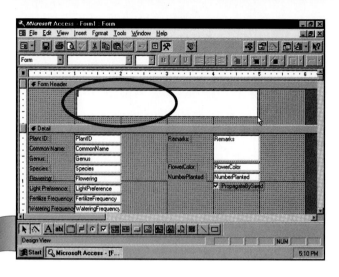

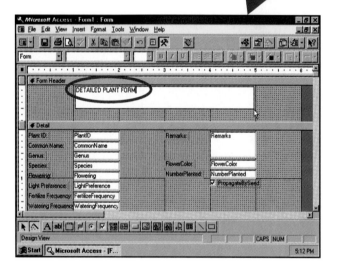

5 Type **DETAILED PLANT FORM**. This is the title for this form. ■

WHY WORRY?

If you decide that you don't want to keep a label box, simply select it and press the Delete key. If your text doesn't fit within the label box, just select the label box and then drag the resize handles until it is the correct size.

TASK 38

Building a Combo Box

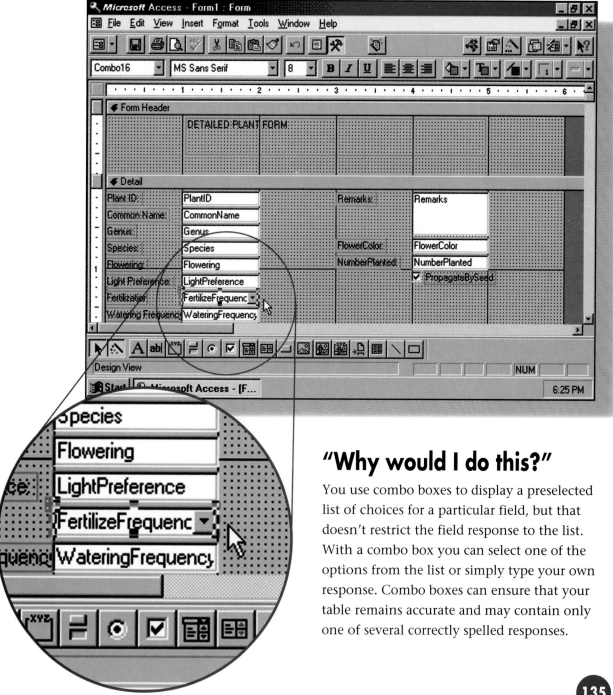

"Why would I do this?"

You use combo boxes to display a preselected list of choices for a particular field, but that doesn't restrict the field response to the list. With a combo box you can select one of the options from the list or simply type your own response. Combo boxes can ensure that your table remains accurate and may contain only one of several correctly spelled responses.

1 Select the field **FertilizeFrequency** on your form. Remember, select a field by clicking the field text box on the right side, not the label.

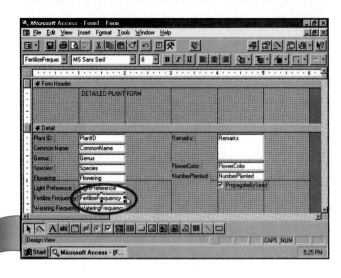

WHY WORRY?

If you accidentally select and delete a field's label box, the field box remains on your form. Simply select and delete the field box in a separate step. A field box can exist without its attached label, but a label can't exist without its field text box.

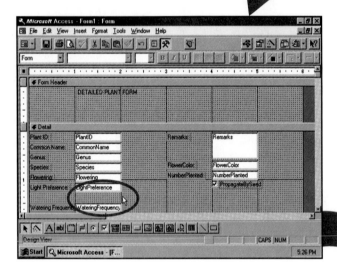

2 Press the **Delete** key. Access removes the field from your form, but does not delete the field from your table. You may want to give yourself more room in the Detail area by dragging the toolbox down to the bottom of your screen if you haven't already done so.

3 Click the **Control Wizards** button on the toolbox and click the **Combo Box** button. Notice how these buttons now appear depressed. A depressed button is a button that you have selected.

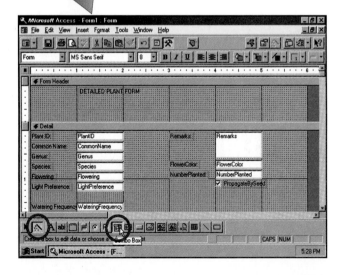

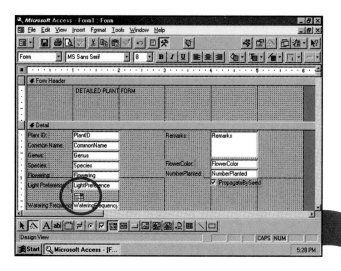

4 Move the mouse pointer to the position where you want to place the combo box and click.

5 The first of several Combo Box Wizard dialog boxes appears. Choose the second option button, **I will type in the values that I want**. Click on the **Next>** button to move to the next dialog box.

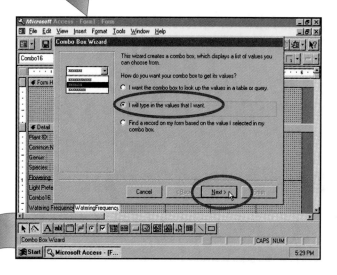

6 Use this dialog box to choose the number of columns for your combo box. This is also where you enter the values to display in the combo box. Press the **Tab** key to move from the text box displaying the number 1 to the first of the column cells.

7 Type **Annually, Spring** in the first row of Col1. Press the **Tab** key again to move to the next cell. Type **Annually, Summer** and press the **Tab** key again. In the next cells type: **Annually**, **Fall**, **Bi-monthly**, **Monthly**, and **Weekly**. Be sure to press the **Tab** key between each entry. Click the **Next>** button to display the next dialog box.

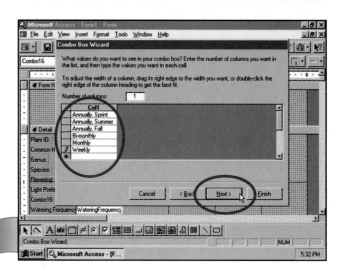

8 This dialog box enables you to decide how the response you select will be used. Choose the second option, **Store that value in this field:**. Select the field **FertilizeFrequency** from the combo box.

WHY WORRY?

Remember, you can always use the Back button to go back to a previous dialog box. You can also use the Cancel button to stop working with a wizard.

9 Click the **Next>** button. Access creates a default label for your combo box. Type **Fertilization Frequency** as the new label for this combo box and then click the **Finish** button to complete and place the field. ■

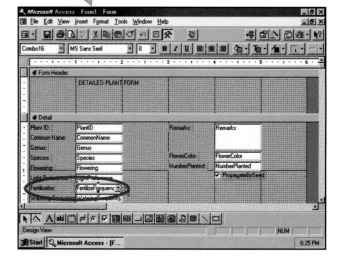

Adding a List Box

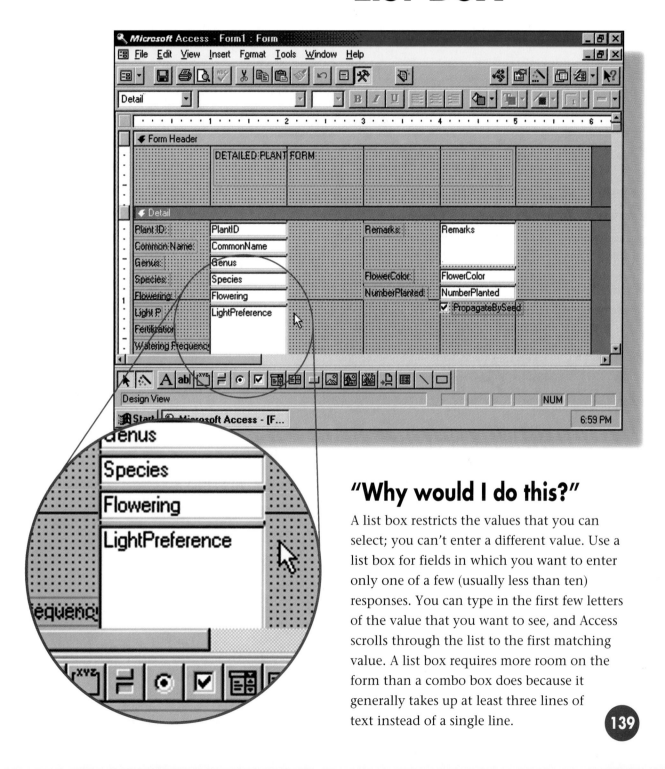

"Why would I do this?"

A list box restricts the values that you can select; you can't enter a different value. Use a list box for fields in which you want to enter only one of a few (usually less than ten) responses. You can type in the first few letters of the value that you want to see, and Access scrolls through the list to the first matching value. A list box requires more room on the form than a combo box does because it generally takes up at least three lines of text instead of a single line.

1 Select the **LightPreference** field. Remember, clicking the field box selects both the field box and the label box.

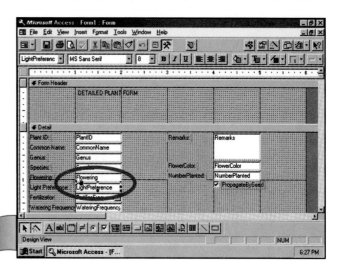

2 Press the **Delete** key to remove the selected field from the form.

WHY WORRY?

If you select the wrong field, or decide you don't want to delete the field, select Edit, Undo Delete from the menu. Access immediately inserts the field back to its previous place. You can't use this function if you use another command after you delete the field.

3 Select the **Control Wizards** button and then click the **List Box** button on toolbox.

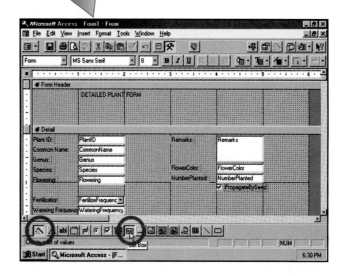

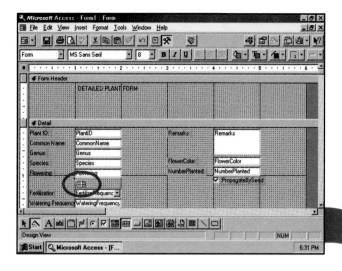

4 Move the mouse pointer, now in the shape of a plus sign with a list box, to the same position as the LightPreference field you just deleted and click the left mouse button once. Access inserts a blank field and displays the first List Box Wizard dialog box.

NOTE ▼

You can resize a field later using its resize handles. Access inserts a field with a default size and shape that varies with each type of field placed on the form.

5 Select the second option button, **I will type in the values that I want**. Click the **Next** button to move to the next dialog box.

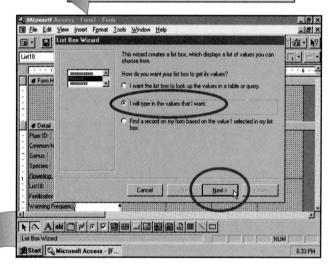

6 The default option of one column works for this field, so press the **Tab** key to move to the first cell in Col1. Remember, you can also move to this cell by moving the mouse pointer to it and clicking once.

7 Type **Full Sun** into this cell and press the **Tab** key to move to the next cell. Type **Filtered Sun** in this cell. Type the remaining values into the subsequent cells, being sure to press the **Tab** key between each. Type **Full Shade**, **Partial Shade**, **Morning Sun**, and **Afternoon Sun**. Click the **Next** button to display the next dialog box.

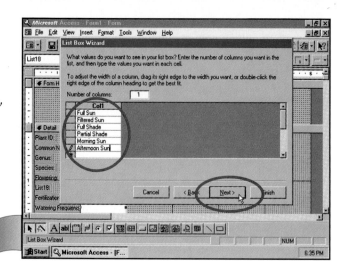

8 Select the second option, **Store that value in this field:** and then choose **LightPreference** from the combo box beside it. Click the **Next>** button to move to the last dialog box.

NOTE ▼

Remember, you can use the Back button to go back to a previous dialog box if you want to change something.

9 Type **Light Preference** into the text box at the top of this dialog box to replace the default label. Click on the **Finish** button, and Access completes the list box and adds it to the form. ■

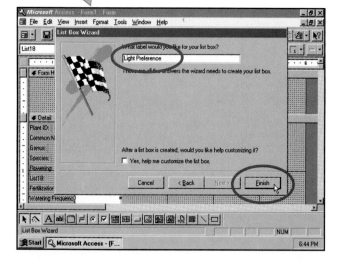

Moving Groups of Objects

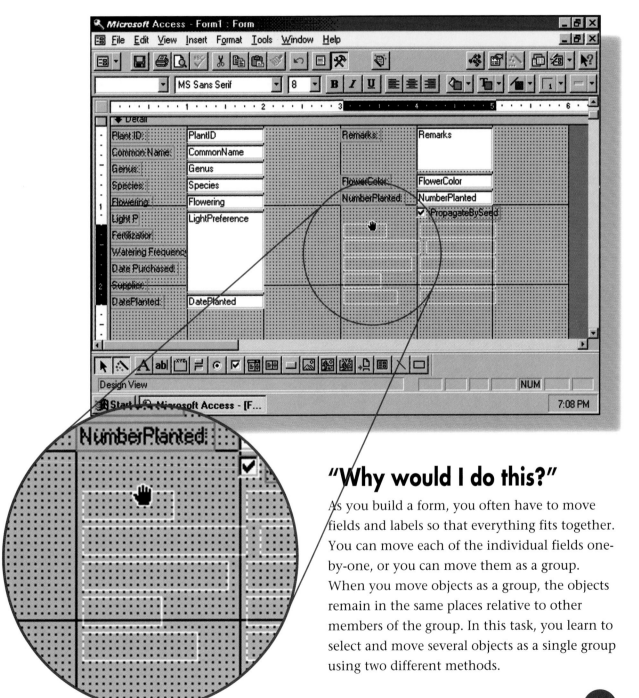

"Why would I do this?"

As you build a form, you often have to move fields and labels so that everything fits together. You can move each of the individual fields one-by-one, or you can move them as a group. When you move objects as a group, the objects remain in the same places relative to other members of the group. In this task, you learn to select and move several objects as a single group using two different methods.

1 Scroll down the screen until you see the bottom half of the form's Detail area.

> **NOTE** ▼
>
> Remember, you can also click the down-arrow button at the bottom of the vertical scroll bar to move the form up your screen.

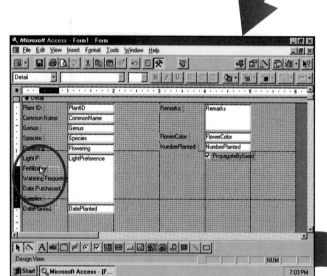

2 Move the mouse pointer to the blank area between the DatePlanted field and its label. Click and drag the mouse pointer up and then to the left until it touches the label text box **Fertilization**. You see that Access draws a rectangle from the point where you first clicked the mouse pointer to its current location.

3 Let go of the mouse button. You now see that you selected all of the field objects and their labels within the rectangle. Even though the rectangle didn't touch any of the field objects, they have also been selected.

> **NOTE** ▼
>
> If you miss a field, just reselect the group again, making a larger selection rectangle.

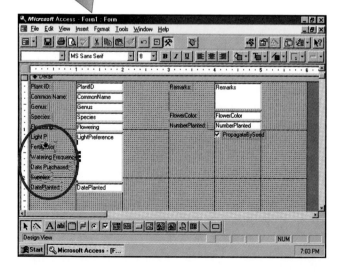

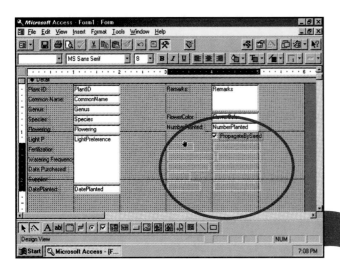

4 Drag these five fields and their labels to the right half of the form.

5 Let go of the mouse button to position the four fields in their new location.

> **NOTE** ▼
>
> You can also select fields that aren't adjacent to each other by pressing and holding the Shift key on your keyboard as you select the fields with the mouse pointer on your screen.

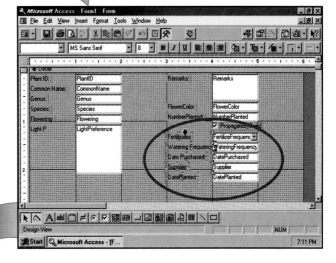

6 Select the **LightPreference** field and drag its bottom resize handle up until it is approximately $3/4$-inch in height. ■

> **WHY WORRY?**
>
> If your fields end up being slightly to one side or the other, just drag them back into the correct place. This can sometimes take a little practice, especially if you have a very sensitive mouse.

Editing a Label

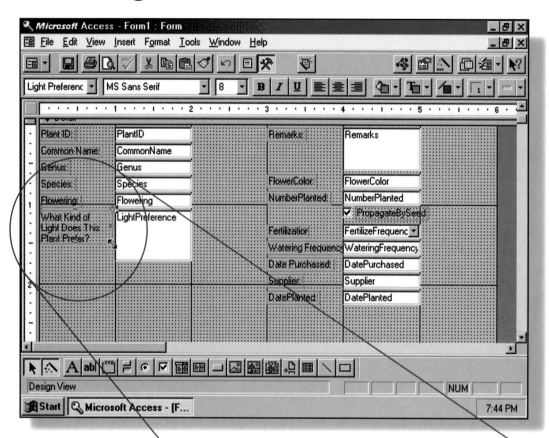

"Why would I do this?"

You may find that some of the labels that you assign to a field don't adequately describe the information that is to go in the field. In order for your form to be of real use to another user, the user should be able to easily infer from the label what data the field requires. With a few simple keystrokes, you can change a field's label. In this task, you learn to change an existing field's label.

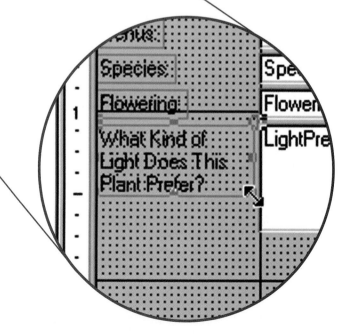

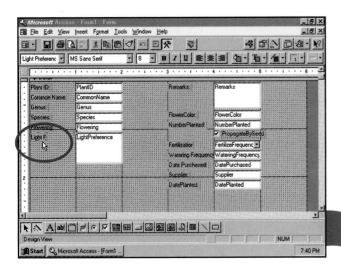

1 Select the **LightPreference** field's label, it now reads Light P. Resize handles appear around the label text box.

2 Press the **Enter** key to switch to edit mode, placing the insertion point at the end of the label's text. Press the **Backspace** key to delete the text in the label box. Type **What Kind of Light Does This Plant Prefer?** into the label text box. Notice how the label stretches across the field object to which it belongs.

WHY WORRY?

You can change the field label text at any time. If you find that a label is confusing, change it.

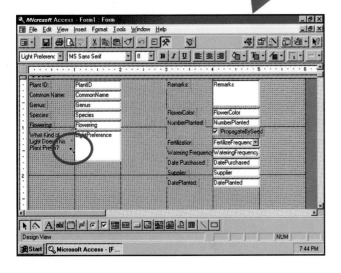

3 Press the **Enter** key to toggle out of the edit mode. Now drag the lower-right corner resize handle to the left and down, so that the lower-right corner of the label box is one gridline to the left of the field object. This creates a label text box that holds three lines of text. Resize the label text box until the text fits neatly within it. ■

Using Toggle Buttons

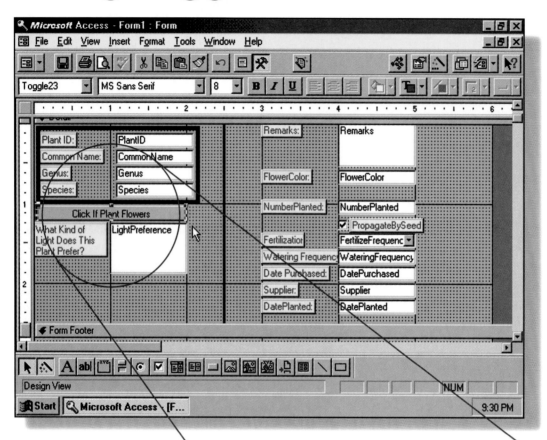

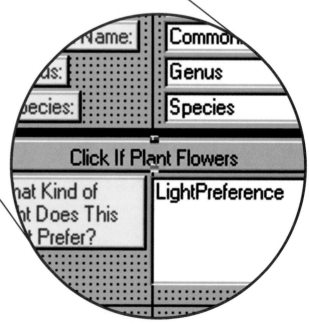

"Why would I do this?"

In a form, you can use a toggle button for any field that requires a simple Yes/No or True/False answer. When you select a toggle button, it is the same as typing "Yes." A toggle button simplifies the process of entering some types of information.

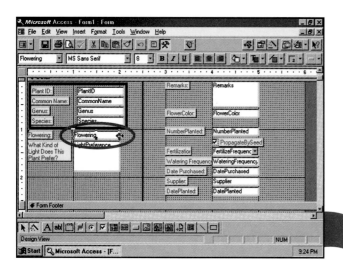

1 Select the field **Flowering** and press the **Delete** key to remove it from your form.

> **NOTE** ▼
>
> Unfortunately, the Toggle Button tool doesn't operate with the Control Wizards like the List and Combo tools. You can use the properties sheet to customize almost any option for this tool by either double-clicking the object or selecting it and then clicking the Properties button.

2 Click the **Toggle Button** on the toolbox. Move the mouse pointer to the form's Detail area where the Flowering field had been located and click once.

> **NOTE** ▼
>
> Option buttons and check boxes are similar to toggle buttons in function, except that you can only use toggle buttons in forms. You can use option buttons and check boxes in both forms and reports. Unlike toggle buttons and check boxes, you can use option buttons to select one of several mutually exclusive responses.

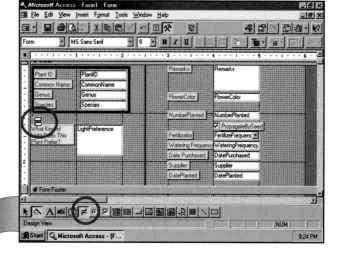

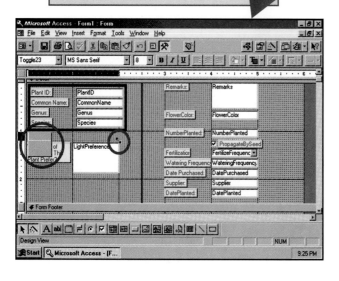

3 You now see a square button appear on your form. Drag the lower-right corner handle so that the button no longer covers the fields below it and stretch it to the two-inch gridline.

4 Click the **Properties** button to display the properties sheet for the new toggle button and press the down-arrow key on your keyboard to move the cursor to the Control Source text box.

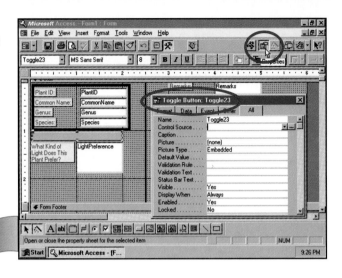

WHY WORRY?

If you make a mistake typing a caption on a button, you can correct this typo by retyping the caption in the Caption text box in the properties sheet, or simply click the caption on the button's face and retype directly on the button.

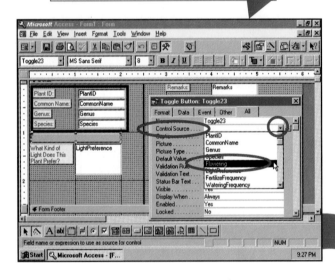

5 Click the arrow button on the end of the text box to display a drop-down list of field objects. Select **Flowering** from this list as the field object; this is the field that controls the toggle button. When you select this button, Access enters a "Yes" response into the Flowering field in the Plants table.

6 Press the down-arrow key once again on your keyboard to move to the Caption text box. Type **Click If Plant Flowers**. Close the properties sheet. You see Access add this caption to the face of your button. ■

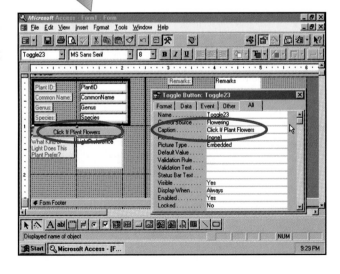

Saving Your New Form

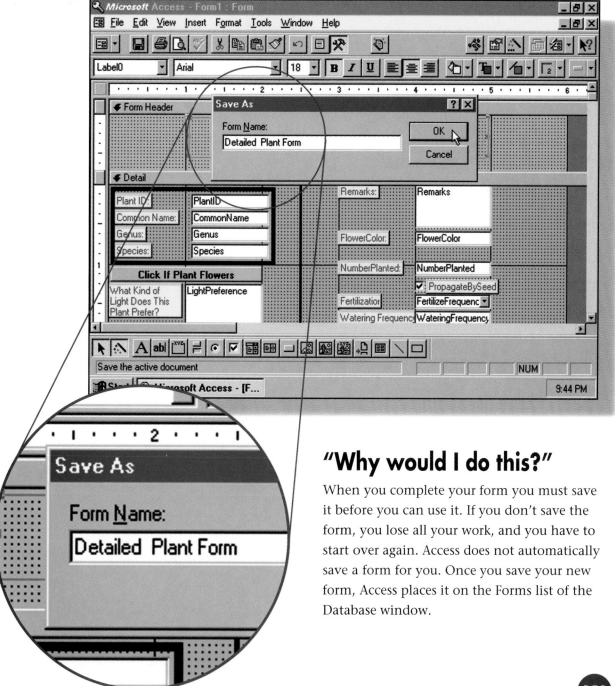

"Why would I do this?"

When you complete your form you must save it before you can use it. If you don't save the form, you lose all your work, and you have to start over again. Access does not automatically save a form for you. Once you save your new form, Access places it on the Forms list of the Database window.

1 Click on the **Save** button on the first toolbar.

NOTE ▼

You can also select File, Save from the menu, or press the keyboard combination Ctrl+S to save a form or other database object.

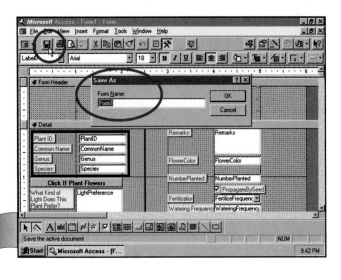

2 Type **Detailed Plant Form** into the text box on the Save As dialog box. This is the name that Access uses to display your form in the Forms list. You can type a new name if you are not happy with the name.

3 Click **OK** and then the **Close** button on the form window. You now see your new form appear in the Forms list of the Database window. ■

WHY WORRY?

Remember, if you find that a form does not meet your needs, you can delete it and create another form, or redesign it in the Form Design view window.

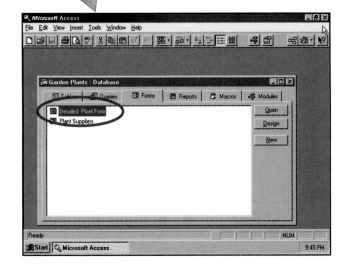

Opening a Form

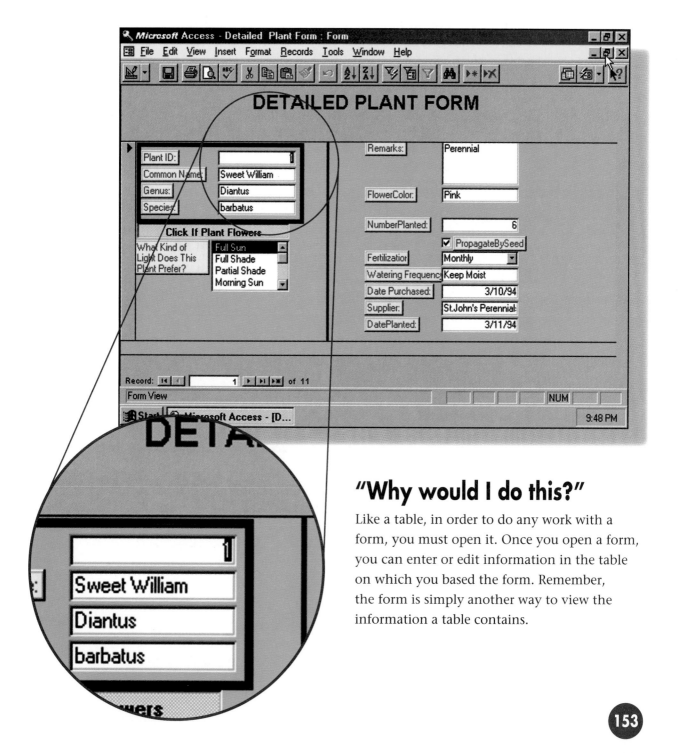

"Why would I do this?"

Like a table, in order to do any work with a form, you must open it. Once you open a form, you can enter or edit information in the table on which you based the form. Remember, the form is simply another way to view the information a table contains.

1 Click on the **Forms** tab in the Database window to display the list of forms in your database.

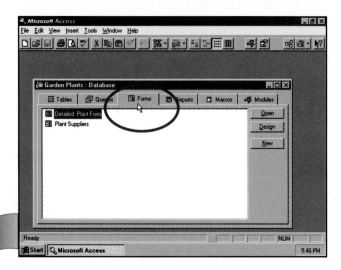

2 Now click on the form name that you want to open. In this example, choose the form **Detailed Plant Form**. Since this is the first form in your list it is automatically selected by default. Click the **Open** button to open your form.

NOTE ▼

You can also use any of the arrow keys on your keyboard, along with the mouse, to select a specific form from the list.

3 Your form appears on-screen. Use the horizontal scroll bar to scroll through the window until you see the upper-right corner of the form window and then click the **Maximize** button so that you can view the form in a larger window. ■

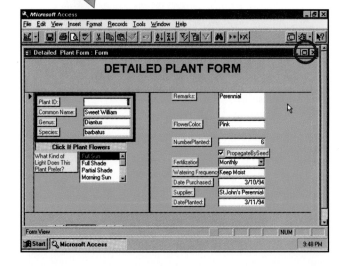

Entering and Editing Information in a Form

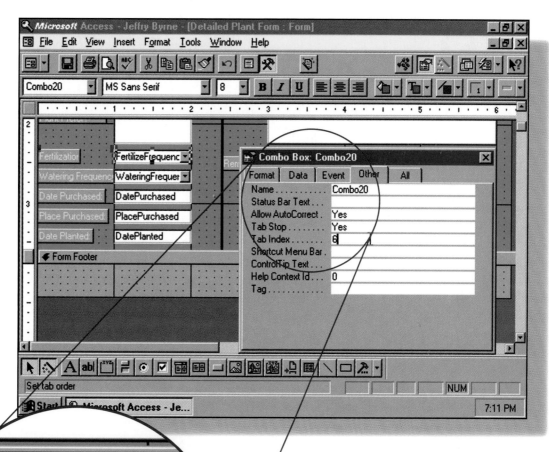

"Why would I do this?"

Using a form to enter new information and to edit old information is more familiar to most people than using a table. If you design a form that looks like a paper form, then transferring information from one to the other is very simple and almost foolproof. When you are more familiar with a format, you are less likely to make mistakes.

1 In order to enter new information in a table, you must get to the next new record line. To quickly display a blank record form click the **New Record** button. It is the rightmost record navigation button located just above the status bar.

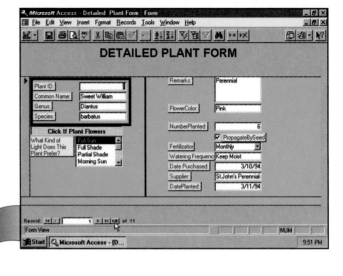

NOTE ▼

You can also open a new record by clicking the New Record button on the toolbar or by selecting Insert, Record from the menu.

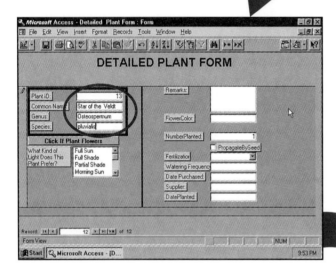

2 Press the **Tab** key to move to the first field, Common Name, and type **Star of the Veldt**. Press the **Tab** key again to move to the next field. Type **Osteospermum** in the Genus field, and **pluvialis** for Species. Be sure to press the **Tab** key to move from field to field.

3 Press the **Tab** key again. The cursor now moves to the Watering Frequency field. Type **Dry Out Between Watering**. Access captures everything you type, even if you can't see it in the field.

NOTE ▼

If you delete a field and then place it again on your form, the field's Tab Index changes. This accounts for the cursor not simply going from one field to the next on your form.

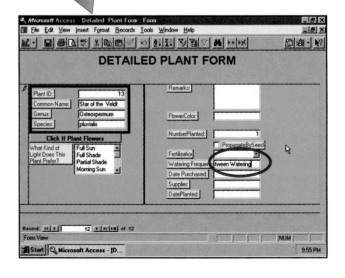

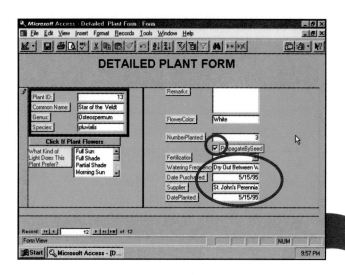

4 Press the **Tab** key once again. Type **5/15/95** in the Date Purchased field and press **Tab**. Type **St. John's Perennials** in the Place Purchased field and press **Tab**. Type **5/15/95** in the Date Planted field. Press the **Tab** key twice to move to the FlowerColor field and type **White**. Press **Tab** again. Enter **3** in the NumberPlanted field. Press **Tab** and then press the **Spacebar** to add a check mark in the PropogateBySeed check box to indicate that you can grow this plant from seed.

5 Press the **Tab** key again to move the cursor to the Fertilization field. Click the arrow button on this combo box field to display a list of options and select **Monthly** from the list.

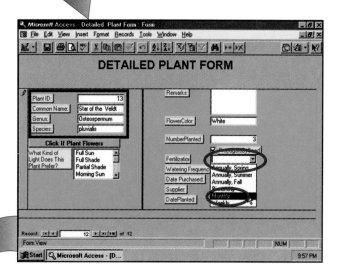

6 Press the **Tab** key to move to the Light Preference list box field and select the option **Full Sun**. To choose a different option you can press the up- or down-arrow keys on your keyboard, or you can use the scroll bar and click an option. The option that is highlighted when you exit the field is the selection that Access enters into the corresponding field in the Plants table.

7 Press the **Tab** key again to move to the Flowering field's toggle button.

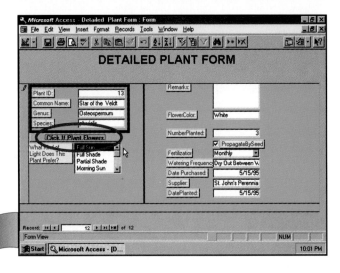

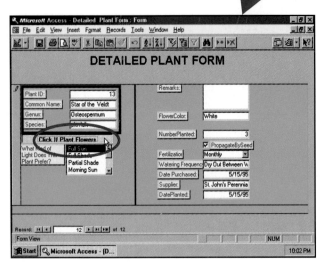

8 Click the **Click If Plant Flowers** button to indicate that this plant does produce flowers. ■

NOTE ▼

You can also press the Spacebar to toggle a button between selected and deselected. When the button appears to be depressed, it is selected.

Changing the Field Order

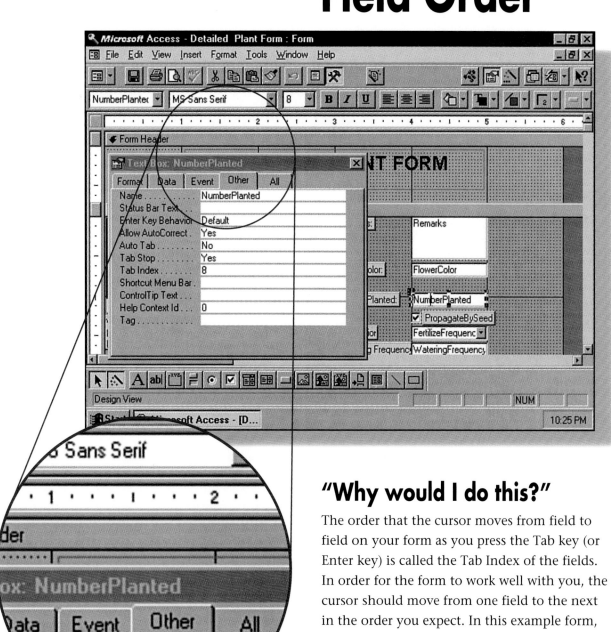

"Why would I do this?"

The order that the cursor moves from field to field on your form as you press the Tab key (or Enter key) is called the Tab Index of the fields. In order for the form to work well with you, the cursor should move from one field to the next in the order you expect. In this example form, you added, deleted, and moved numerous fields. When you add and delete fields, the Tab Index of your fields changes.

1 Click the **Form View** button. The form appears in Form View.

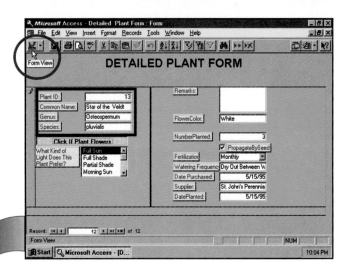

2 Select the **Plant ID** field on your form. Click the **Properties** button on the first toolbar to display the properties sheet for this field.

3 Click the **Other** tab on the properties sheet. This limits the display to only a few properties, including the Tab Index and Tab Stop properties.

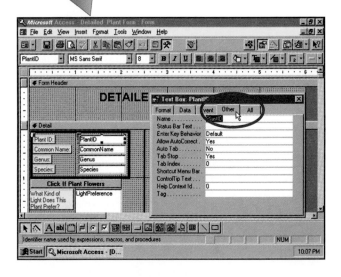

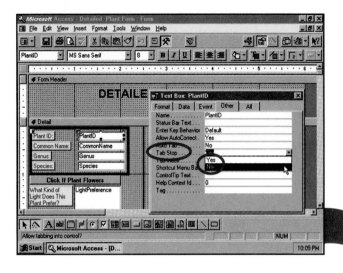

4 Move the cursor down to the **Tab Stop** text box and change this option from Yes to **No**. The Tab Stop property determines whether the cursor passes through this field or not. When set to Yes, the cursor moves to the field when you press the Tab key.

NOTE ▼

The Plant ID field is an AutoNumber data type, so you can't change this field. Setting this property to No causes Access to bypass the field. In an editable field, you can use the mouse to move into the field.

5 After you set the Tab Stop property to No, you don't need to worry about the Tab Index setting. The first field always appears with a Tab Index setting of 0. Use the mouse pointer to select the **CommonName** field. The Tab Stop is set to Yes, and the Tab Index is set to 1. These settings don't require changes.

6 Continue to select each field object in the order that you want to select the fields when you press the Tab key. Check the Tab Index number for each field to make sure that the number is one larger than the previous field. Access automatically adjusts all of the remaining field's Tab Index numbers.

7 Change the **LightPreference** field's Tab Index from 14 to **5**.

> **NOTE** ▼
>
> Access does not enable you to create duplicate Tab Index numbers. For example, if you change Tab Index 10 to 3, then the field that had had Tab Index 3 would automatically become 4. The field that had been 9 would now be 10.

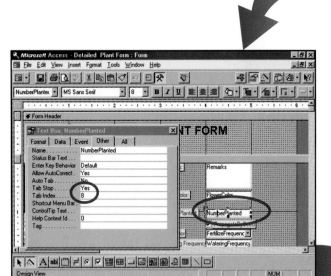

8 Change the Tab Index property as indicated: Remarks, **6**; FlowerColor, **7**; NumberPlanted, **8**; PropagateBySeed, **9**; and FertilizeFrequency, **10**. The remaining fields shouldn't need to be changed.

9 Click the **Form View** button again and test the new Tab Index order of your form. The form opens with the first record in your table. The cursor is in the Common Name field instead of the Plant ID field. Press the **Tab** key to move through each field with a Tab Index. Be sure to click the **Save** button to save the changes made to the form. ■

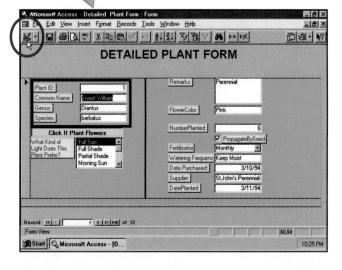

PART V

Getting Information from a Database

So far, you have learned to design, build, and use a table to store information. You then found out how to create a form that you can use to display, add, and edit data in the table on which you based the form. Gathering and storing information in an organized fashion is fine, but those tasks are only half the reason for collecting the data. You must also be able to find that information and make decisions based on it. One of the most powerful features included with Access is your ability to ask questions about the information you collect.

A question is built in the form of an example and is called a *query*. Unlike a simple card file where you can look up one record at a time, Access can respond to a query by finding all records that meet certain examples, called *criteria*. Criteria are simply restrictions on the information that Access includes in its search. For example, you can query Access to find the records of all of your suppliers who are based in California; the criterion is that a record must include the abbreviation *CA* in the state field. The process of building a query in this fashion is known as *query by example*, or QBE for short.

You can also create queries that are quite complex, such as "Show me the records of all customers who purchased items A, B, and C more than twice in the past year" or "Create a list of all suppliers who are not based in New York." Writing out your query as a simple question or statement helps you to focus on what information you are looking for. Queries like these can help you focus your attention on specific details or trends in your business.

Criteria can include more than one field or table. For example, you can construct a query that finds and displays all customers who live in California or New York and who have bought more than $500 worth of merchandise in the past year.

Some of the tasks for which you can design a query are:

- Showing records that meet specified criteria

- Displaying selected data from a table, sorted in a specific order

- Updating specific fields in selected records with new information

- Displaying selected records from several tables at once

- Adding information from one table to another

- Deleting selected information or records from a table

You can create several different types of queries, each of which produces a different result. The most commonly used are:

Select Query   This type of query enables you to specify various criteria for Access to use in selecting records. All of the selected records are then displayed in the Datasheet View of the query.

Crosstab Query   This type of query is often used to graph information from a table or tables. You create a Crosstab query to display trends and generate summaries of information about groups of records. There is a Crosstab Wizard that you use to help you create this type of query. It is often used to compare one aspect of your records to another.

Action Query   This type of query is used to add information to, or edit information in, a group of records in either an existing table or a new table. For example, you can use an action query to update the prices of items that you sell, or to delete all customers who have not purchased products in the last two years.

Once you create and run a query, you can use the resulting datasheet in a form or report. You can build a query that uses information from several tables. For example, you can combine information from a Sales table and a Customer table to find out who your best customers are. Basing a report on a query ensures that the report has the most up-to-date information. You can easily build a query that selects all customers who have past-due invoices. Then use the resulting datasheet to create a report that lists these customers, their phone numbers, the invoices that are past due, and display a subtotal for each customer.

When you begin to build queries, write them down in either a question or statement form. The simple task of putting a question on paper helps you to focus on what you are looking for, and also helps you to revise a query if you don't get the answer or format you were expecting. Be as specific as possible in building your query statement and refine it if necessary. The more specific you are when you write your question, the easier the job of building the actual query is.

Building a Select Query

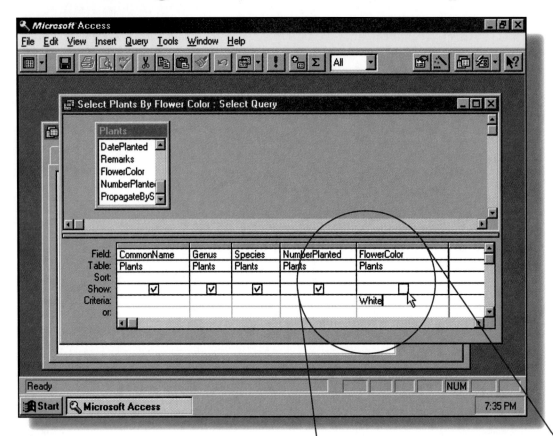

"Why would I do this?"

The select query is the most common type of query. You use this query to select records that meet your specified criteria, and then display them in a datasheet. For example, you can build a query for the statement, "Display all records for plants that have white flowers, and include only the Common Name, Genus, Species, and Number Planted."

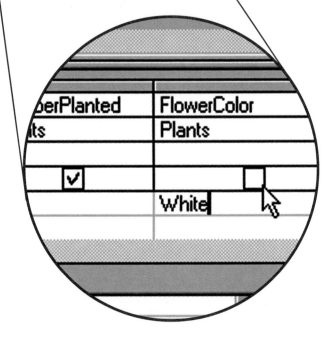

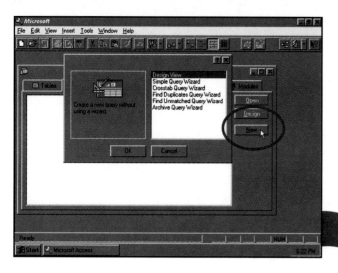

1 Open the **Garden Plants** database file. On the Database window, click the **Queries** tab. You see a blank Query list. Just like the Table and Forms list, once you build and save a query, Access lists it here. Click the **New** button on the Database window. You see the New Query dialog box.

2 Be sure that the option **Design View** is selected in the list box; then click the **OK** button. The Show Table dialog box displays on top of the Select Query window. Select the **Plants** table from the list box in the Show Table dialog box and then click the **Add** button.

NOTE ▼

If you plan to base a query on the results of another query, click the Queries tab on the Show Table dialog box. Selecting the Both tab enables you to choose either tables or queries from the list box.

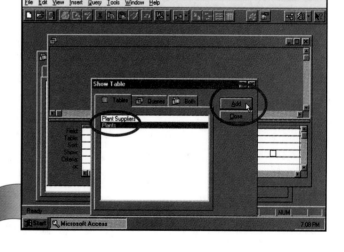

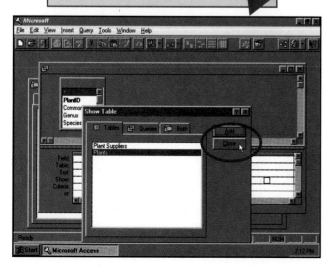

3 Close the Show Table dialog box by clicking the **Close** button. If you are creating a query that is to be based on multiple tables, select the tables before closing Show Table. You then see each table or query listed in the Query window.

169

4 In the Plants table list box, select the first field to be included in the query by double-clicking the field **CommonName**. Access immediately places that field in the first column of the query grid. You can select all fields for a query in this manner.

NOTE ▼

To include all fields in the query, double-click the asterisk (*) above the other field names. Access adds a single column to include all of the fields. To sort or specify other criteria, you can add a second copy of those specific fields.

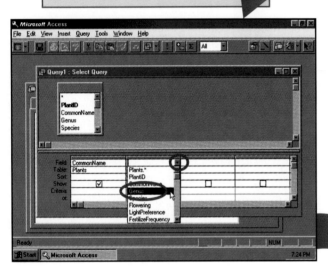

5 Click the mouse pointer in the Field row of the second column of the query grid and click the arrow button that you see at the end of the field. From the drop-down list of field names that appears, choose the field **Genus** as the second field for this query. Add the **Species** and **NumberPlanted** fields as the third and fourth columns using either method from step 4 or 5.

6 Select the **FlowerColor** field and double-click it—but where is it? You can scroll through the grid with the horizontal scroll bar at the bottom of the window, or resize the columns. Place the mouse pointer on the right edge of each of the column selector buttons and double-click. The columns automatically change to best fit the information in them.

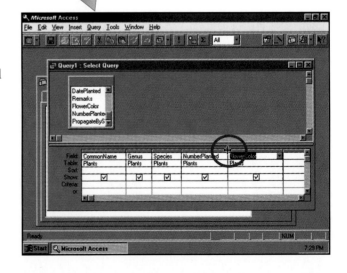

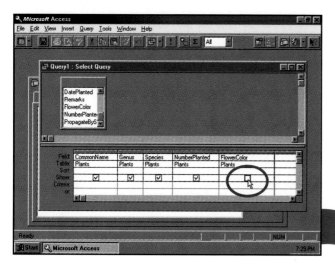

7 Click the check box in the row labeled **Show** in the FlowerColor column. This removes the check mark, indicating to Access that you do not want to show this field in the resulting datasheet.

WHY WORRY?

You can always click the Show check box again, so that the field appears in the resulting datasheet.

8 Press the down arrow key, moving the cursor to the Criteria row in the FlowerColor column, and type **White**. This is the actual criterion that any selected records must meet—they must have white, and only white, flowers.

NOTE ▼

Of course, you can also move the mouse pointer to the Criteria row and click in order to move the cursor to this cell of the query grid.

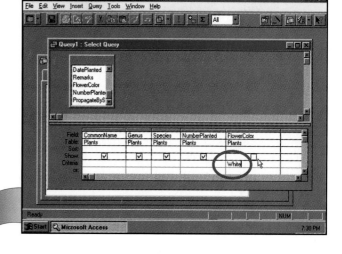

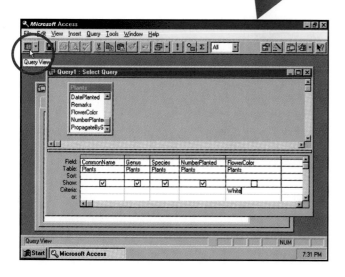

9 Display the answer for this query in a datasheet by clicking either the **Run**, or **Query View** button on the toolbar (both buttons perform the same function in a select query). For action queries, the Query View button shows you the records that Access selects and acts upon, while the Run button actually performs the job specified in the action query.

10 You can save the query so you can use it again later. Click the **Close** button on the datasheet's window. You see a dialog box asking if you want to save this query statement. Select the **Yes** button.

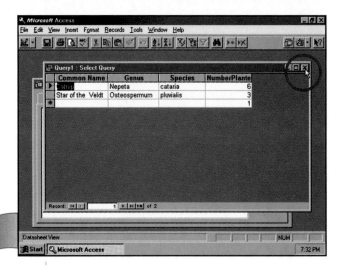

11 Type **Select Plants By Flower Color** in the text box of the **Save As** dialog box and click the **OK** button to save the query with this name.

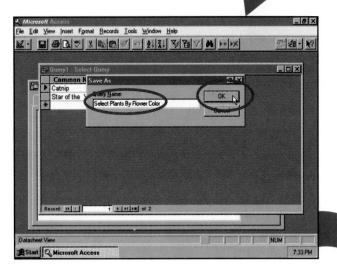

WHY WORRY?

If the query did not perform as you thought, simply click the Query View button again to return to the Query Design View window. You can make adjustments to the query statement and then view the results again.

12 You see Access add the new query to the Queries list in the Database window. You can easily use this query to choose plants with colors other than white, by simply changing the color criteria from "White" to any other color that you may want to see in the Query Design View window. ■

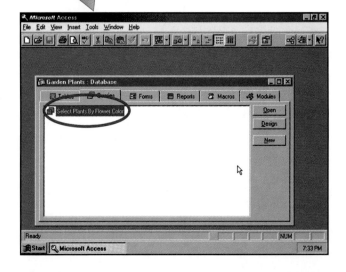

TASK 48

Using a Crosstab Query

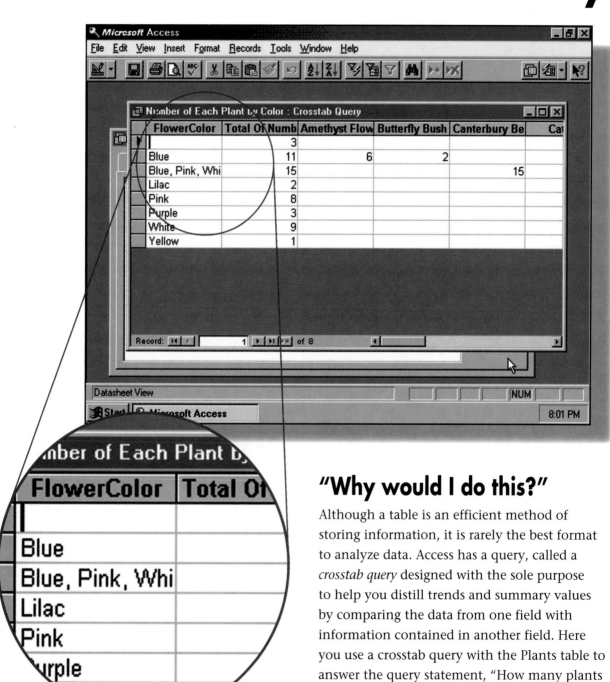

"Why would I do this?"

Although a table is an efficient method of storing information, it is rarely the best format to analyze data. Access has a query, called a *crosstab query* designed with the sole purpose to help you distill trends and summary values by comparing the data from one field with information contained in another field. Here you use a crosstab query with the Plants table to answer the query statement, "How many plants of each color do I have planted?"

173

1 Open the Query list by clicking the **Queries** tab on the Database window. Click the **New** button, displaying the New Query dialog box, and choose **Crosstab Query Wizard** from the list. Click the **OK** button.

> **NOTE** ▼
> Remember, you can also begin a new query by either pressing Ctrl+N on your keyboard, or selecting Insert, Query from the menu.

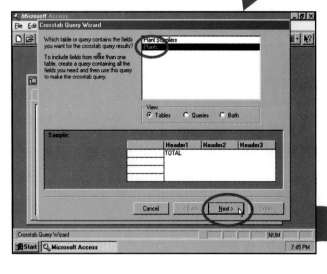

2 Here you see the first Crosstab Query Wizard dialog box. Like building a query from scratch, Access selects the Tables option by default. Select the **Plants** table from the list and click the **Next>** button.

> **NOTE** ▼
> You can also simply double-click the Crosstab Query Wizard option in the list box to both select it and launch the wizard.

3 In this dialog box you choose the fields to use as row headings. You want to find plants by color, so select the field **FlowerColor** and click the **>** button. You see the field move from the Available Fields list to the Selected Fields list. Click the **Next>** button.

> **NOTE** ▼
> You can choose a maximum of three fields for your row headers, enabling you to sort and group fields together.

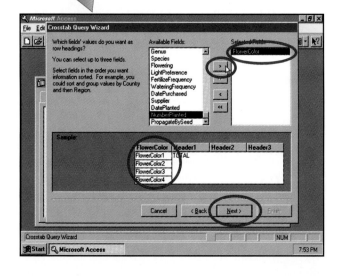

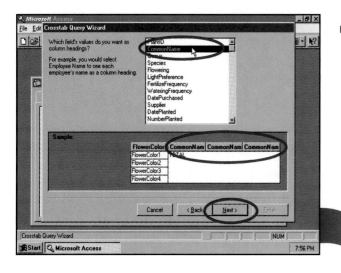

4 Here you choose the field that acts as the column heading. To compare flower color to plants you can use either Genus or Common Name to identify your plants. Select the field **CommonName** for this query; it is possible to have several plants share the same Genus name, but not the same common name. Click the **Next>** button.

5 Choose the summary calculation you want to display, on what field, and if you want to see a separate column that will give you total sums on each row. Click the check box **Yes, include row sums**, select the field **NumberPlanted** from the Fields list box, and choose the **Sum** function. The calculated expression appears in the sample box. Click the **Next>** button.

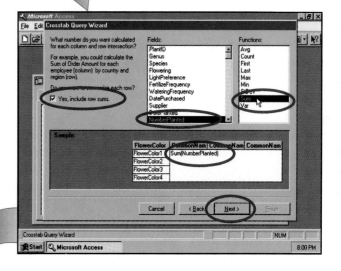

6 Type **Number of Each Plant by Color**. You don't need to make any other changes in this dialog box. Select the **Finish** button.

7 The datasheet shows each of the various colors that you've entered into the FlowerColor field of the Plants table. One plant, Costmary, has no flower color listed; this means that either it doesn't flower, or you did not enter the information. The column labeled Total Of NumberPlanted (widen the column to see the whole name) shows you the total number of plants of each color that you planted.

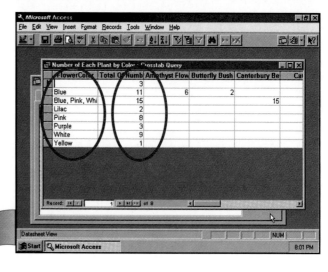

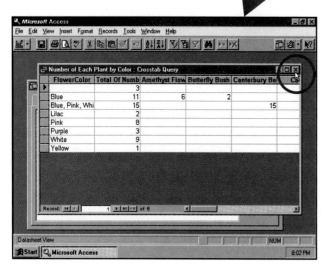

8 Click the **Close** button to close the datasheet and save the new query. It now appears on your Queries list. ■

> **NOTE** ▼
>
> The field(s) you select for row headings do not appear as choices for column headings. This occurs because you cannot create a comparison of something to itself.

Selecting Records with Wild Cards

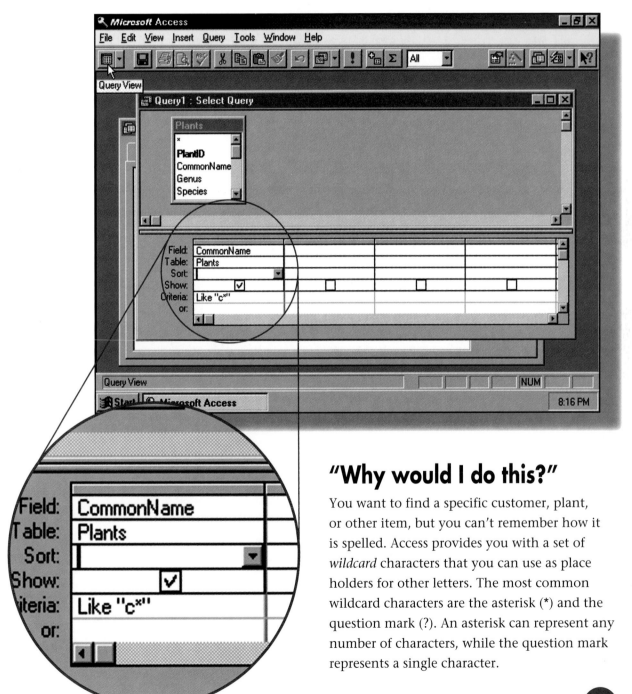

"Why would I do this?"

You want to find a specific customer, plant, or other item, but you can't remember how it is spelled. Access provides you with a set of *wildcard* characters that you can use as place holders for other letters. The most common wildcard characters are the asterisk (*) and the question mark (?). An asterisk can represent any number of characters, while the question mark represents a single character.

1 Open the **Queries** list and select the **New** button. Choose **Design View** from the list and click the **OK** button. You now see the Show Table dialog box and a blank Select Query window behind it.

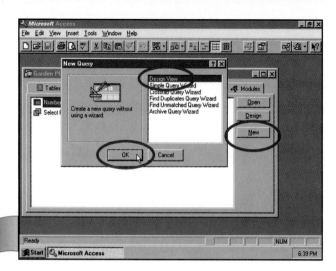

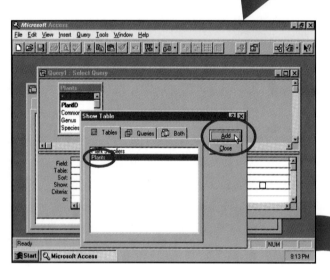

2 Select the **Plants** table from the list in the Show Table dialog box and click the **Add** button. The Plants field list appears in the Select Query window. Click the **Close** button on the Show Table dialog box.

NOTE ▼

Remember, you can also double-click the table, or query name, to both select it and add it to the Query window.

3 Double-click the field **CommonName** to add it to the query grid. Move the cursor down to the Criteria row in the same column.

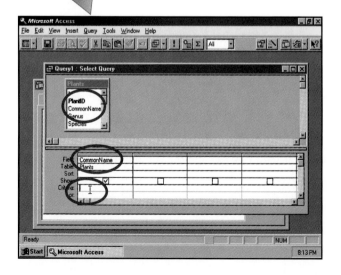

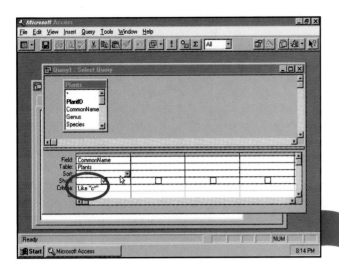

4 Type **c***. This criterion tells Access to search for and display all plants with a common name that begins with the letter C. Press an arrow key, or click the mouse pointer in another cell of the grid. Notice that Access changes the criterion to read Like "c*".

NOTE ▼

When using a wildcard character in a query criteria, you don't have to be case-specific. Access considers a lowercase letter "c" to be the same as an uppercase "C."

5 Click the **Query View** button on the toolbar. Access displays the datasheet for this query with any records found. If no records are found, a blank datasheet displays.

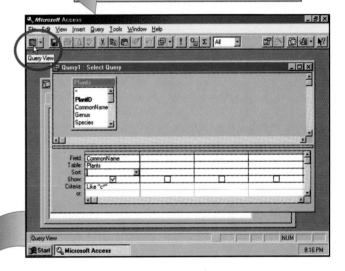

WHY WORRY?

If you don't find the information you're seeking, look at your query statement again. If it's correct, you may want to manually check for records in the table that do meet your criteria— to ensure that they do in fact exist.

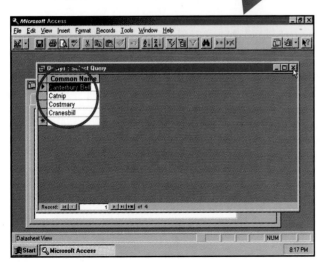

6 Close the datasheet window by clicking the **Close** button and then select the **No** button in the Save dialog box that appears. ■

Selecting Records with an "OR" Criteria

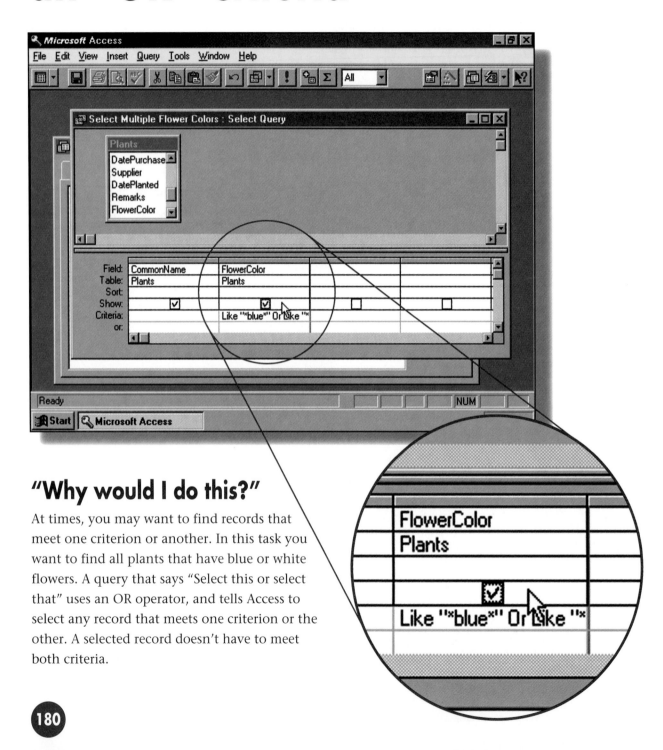

"Why would I do this?"

At times, you may want to find records that meet one criterion or another. In this task you want to find all plants that have blue or white flowers. A query that says "Select this or select that" uses an OR operator, and tells Access to select any record that meets one criterion or the other. A selected record doesn't have to meet both criteria.

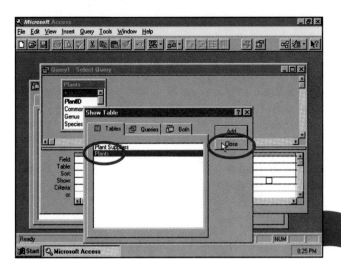

1 Open the **Queries** list and select the **New** button. Choose **New Query** from the list and then the **OK** button. Double-click the **Plants** table for this query and then **Close** the Show Table dialog box.

2 Double-click the field **CommonName** from the list. Now scroll down the field list and select the field **FlowerColor** and add it to the grid by double-clicking it.

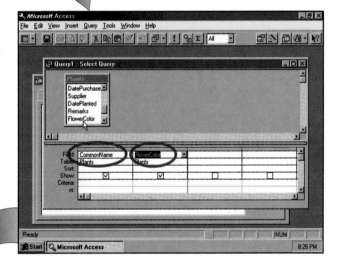

3 Move the cursor down to the Criteria row of the FlowerColor column and type, **"*blue*" OR "*white*"** and then press the up arrow key. The wildcard asterisks are used so that any plants with multiple flower colors—including white or blue—appear. Access adds the word "Like" with the wildcard characters.

4 Click the **Query View** button to display the datasheet for this query.

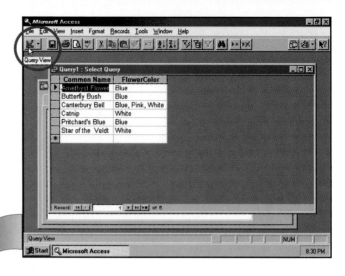

> **NOTE** ▼
>
> An "OR" criterion can be broken into two parts and placed in separate criteria rows. Notice that the row below the Criteria row is labeled "or." You could type the first criteria "*blue*" in the Criteria row and then type the second criteria "*white*" into the second row.

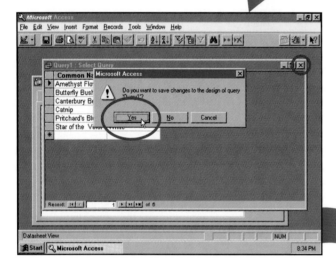

5 Click the **Close** button on the datasheet window and then the **Yes** button on the next dialog box.

6 Save this query using the name **Select Multiple Flower Colors** in the Save As dialog box and then click the **OK** button. You now see Access add the new query to the Queries list. ■

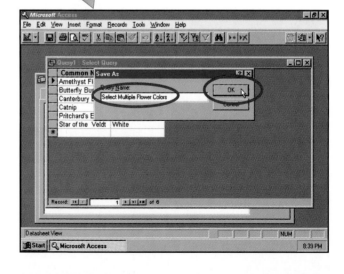

Selecting Records That Match More Than One Criterion

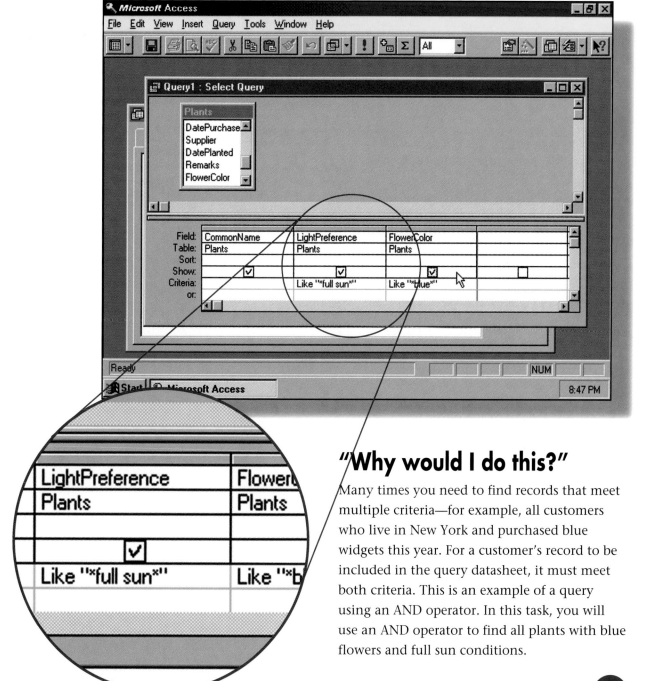

"Why would I do this?"

Many times you need to find records that meet multiple criteria—for example, all customers who live in New York and purchased blue widgets this year. For a customer's record to be included in the query datasheet, it must meet both criteria. This is an example of a query using an AND operator. In this task, you will use an AND operator to find all plants with blue flowers and full sun conditions.

1 Open the **Queries** list and select the **New** button. Choose **New Query** and click the **OK** button. Add the Plants table to the query grid by selecting **Plants** and click on **Add**. Then, close the Show Table dialog box.

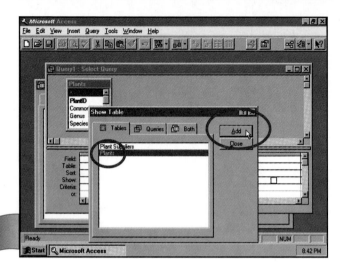

2 Select these fields (by double-clicking on them) from the Plants list and add each to the query grid: **CommonName**, **LightPreference**, and **FlowerColor**.

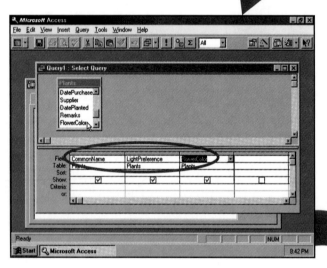

3 Move the cursor to the **Criteria** row of the LightPreference column and type "***full sun***". Move the cursor to the **Criteria** row of the FlowerColor column and type "***blue***", then move the cursor from this cell. The asterisk wildcards include the possibilities of plants that have more than one choice entered into a field.

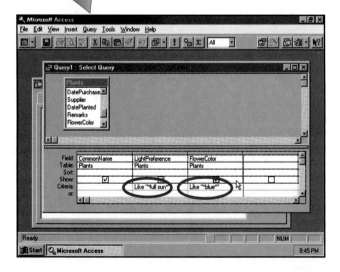

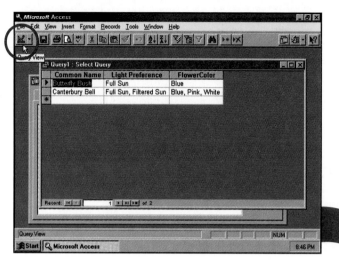

4 Click the **Query View** button to see the resulting datasheet. Two records meet these criteria; notice how the second record would've been excluded without the wildcards having been used.

NOTE ▼

Whenever you want to select records using the "AND" operator, place both criteria on the same row. Placing criteria in separate rows for different fields will be interpreted by Access as an "OR" operator.

5 Click the **Close** button and then the **No** button on the dialog box so that you don't save this query. ■

WHY WORRY?

If your query datasheet includes records that don't meet both criteria you entered, check the query grid again. Be sure that you entered both criteria on the same row and didn't accidentally create an "OR" query instead.

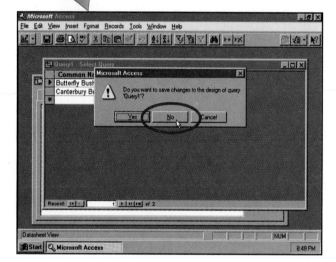

Using Arithmetic Operators

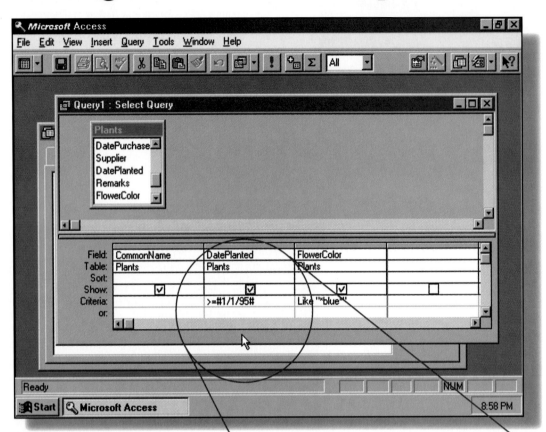

"Why would I do this?"

Arithmetic operators can be used for both text or numeric data types. For example, you can use an arithmetic operator in a query to display records for customers with last names beginning with the letter F to the letter M. The most commonly used arithmetic operators include = (equal), < (less than), > (greater than), <= (less than or equal to), and >= (greater than or equal to). In this task, create a query displaying plants with blue flowers that were planted on or after January 1, 1995.

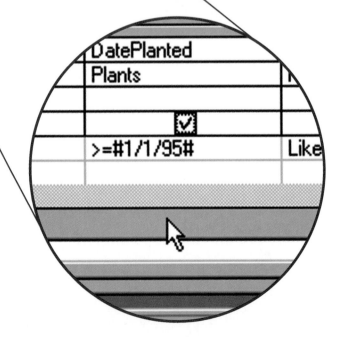

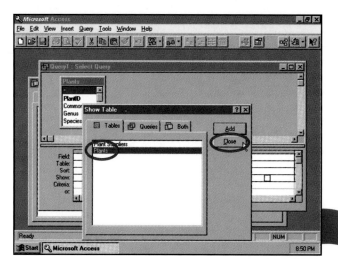

1 Open the **New Query** dialog box, choose **New Query** from the list, and click the **OK** button. Select the **Plants** table for this query and then close the Show Table dialog box.

2 From the Plants field list select **CommonName**, **DatePlanted**, and **FlowerColor**.

> **NOTE** ▼
>
> Since this query requires the answer to meet both criteria, the query uses an AND operator. Be sure you enter both criteria in the same row.

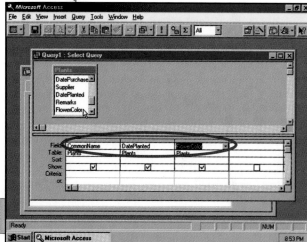

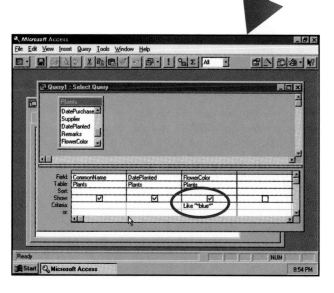

3 The first part of the query statement is "display all plants that have blue flowers." Move the cursor to the Criteria row in the **FlowerColor** column and type, **"*blue*"**. Access changes the criteria to read Like "*blue*", once you move the cursor from the cell.

4 Move the cursor to the Criteria row in the **DatePlanted** column. Type **>=1/1/95** into the criteria cell and then press the up arrow key. Notice how Access changes this entry to read >=#1/1/95#. The # symbols indicate that the numbers between them are a date.

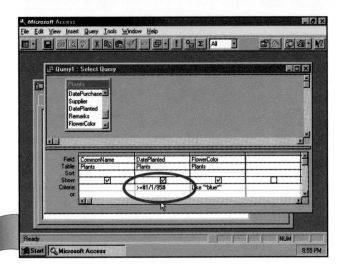

5 Click the **Query View** button to view the resulting datasheet for this query.

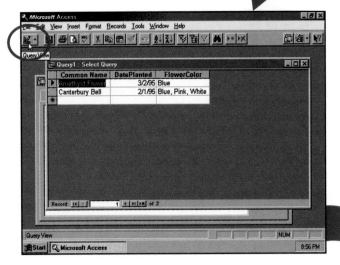

6 Close this window without saving it, by clicking the **Close** button and then the **No** button in the displayed dialog box. ■

WHY WORRY?

If your query displays records that meet one or the other criterion, you may have built an "OR" query by entering the criteria on separate lines. Make sure that the criteria statements are in the same line to create an "AND" query.

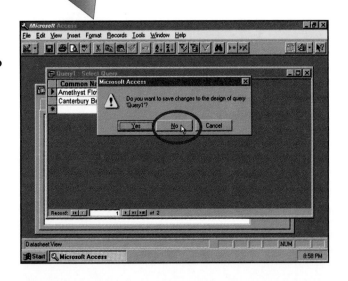

PART VI

Creating and Using Reports

U p to now, you designed and used tables to store data; forms to view, enter, and edit data; and finally, queries to select information. These skills alone are fine if you never have to share your information with a co-worker. Those situations seldom occur in the real world, however, so you also need to know how to create a printed report.

While you can print copies of your tables, forms, and results of a query, you have much greater control over the format of information with a printed report. In many ways, building a report is similar to designing a form: you can choose how to group records with the report, select fields to include, and decide on the placement of fields within the report. Most of the techniques that you learned in order to design a form also apply directly to designing a report. You can also create a report that displays subtotals for selected groups of records, or for each page, and then include a final total for the entire report at the end. When you build a report, you can easily add summary information, such as totals, subtotals, and percentages, for groups of records, or the complete report.

Often, you create a query and then base the report on the information presented by the query. This enables you to have a great deal of control over the information that you include in your report.

You can create reports for a variety of purposes, including:

- Mailing labels
- Invoices
- Product shelf tags
- Address and phone lists
- Analysis of sales and purchases
- Lists of sales contacts
- Account-collections letters

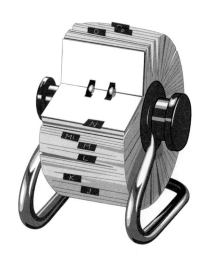

You can create a report by using either a Report Wizard or by building your report from the Report Design View window. A report you create with a Report Wizard can use more than one table, unlike earlier versions of Access. There are three Report Wizards and two AutoReports that you can choose from to help you easily build a report:

Report Wizard   This wizard enables you to create a report with the greatest degree of control. You can choose more than one table or query on which to base the report, and select only the fields that you want to display. You can also choose to group records by a specific field(s), and how to sort records within a group. You can print the report in either portrait or landscape mode and you have a choice of six different field layouts, or styles, with this wizard.

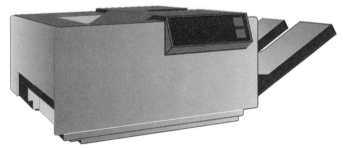

Chart Wizard   This wizard creates a report that displays a chart, or graph, of information selected from tables or queries. You can choose from 12 chart styles.

Label Wizard   The Label Wizard enables you to print on many standard size labels for either continuous feed or sheet feed printers. You can use these labels as mailing labels, product labels, or any other kind of label.

AutoReport: Columnar   This report is very similar in structure to the AutoForm. Each field appears inside of a box, with its label displayed to the left.

AutoReport: Tabular   This report displays all field labels at the top of each page of the report with the records below. Each page displays as many records as fit on the page—this varies depending upon the types of fields in the selected table or query. If all of the fields can't fit across a single page, then Access displays the remaining fields on page two, with the next group of records being printed on page three.

While these reports are usable, more often than not you may want to make some changes to the design of these reports rather than using them straight out of the can. You can easily edit the design of any report by opening it in the Report Design View window.

Reports can include color and reverse printing—white text on a black background. Use these options with discretion. Color and reverse printing works best if you can print the report with a color inkjet or laser printer. If you use a dot matrix printer, limit yourself to text and lines or your report may not be legible.

Building a Report with a Wizard

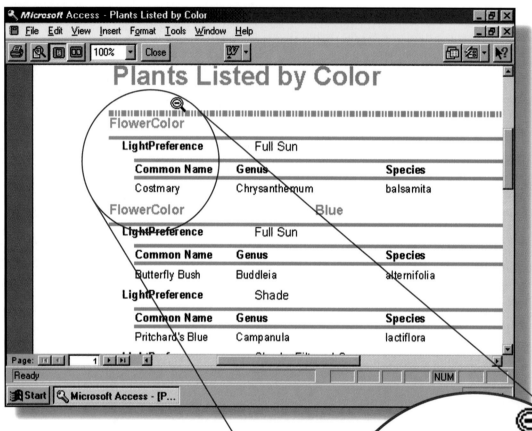

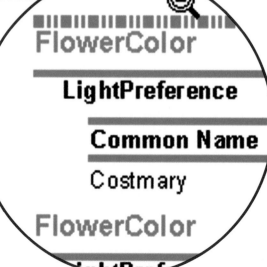

"Why would I do this?"

You set up your tables, created forms, learned to use queries, and entered information into your tables. Now the boss wants a report on her desk by quitting time today. By using the Report Wizard, you can quickly create a report with a polished, professional appearance.

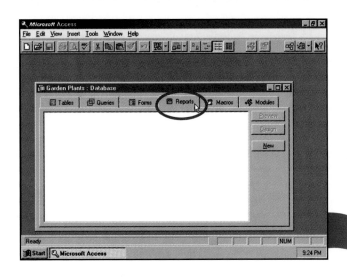

1 Click the **Reports** tab on the Database window. Notice that the Reports list is blank. Like tables, forms, and queries, Access adds each new report that you build and save to this list.

> **NOTE** ▼
>
> Remember, you can use the **>>** button to select all of the field names at once and move them to the Selected Fields list box.

2 Click the **New** button. You see the New Report dialog box appear. Select **Report Wizard** from the list box. Click the arrow button on the next list box and choose **Plants** from the combo box (this is the table that you want to use for this report). This combo box displays all of the tables and queries in the database. Click the **OK** button.

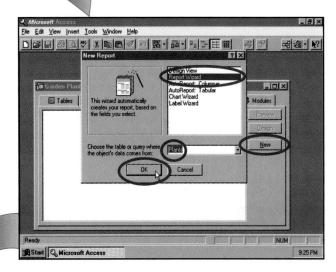

3 Use this Report Wizard dialog box to choose the fields to include. Choose **CommonName**, **Genus**, **Species**, **LightPreference**, and **FlowerColor** as the fields, clicking the **>** button after you select each field. Click the **Next>** button.

4 Use this dialog box to choose how you want to group the records. Select **FlowerColor** and **LightPreference** as the fields by which to group your records. These choices tell Access to group your records by the color of the plant's flowers. Within each group, Access then subdivides the records by light preference. Click the **Next>** button.

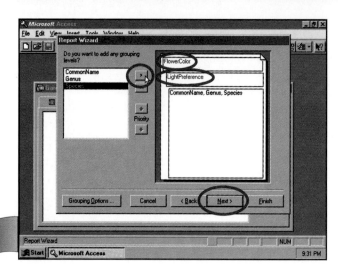

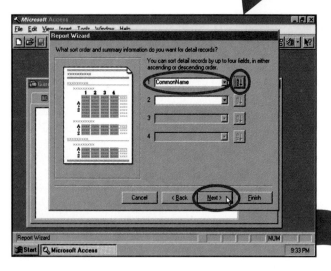

5 This dialog box enables you to select a field and set up the options to sort the detail records of your report. The detail records are those that you are not using to group your records. Click the arrow button and choose the **CommonName** field. Select the sort order by clicking the button to the right of the combo box; the default is ascending (from A through Z). Click the **Next>** button again.

6 Click each of the Layout option buttons to view the sample layouts. Select the **Outline 1** option button. Click the **Next>** button.

NOTE ▼

If you have more than eight fields in your report, you may want to choose to print in landscape orientation. Access then prints the report across your page, instead of down the page.

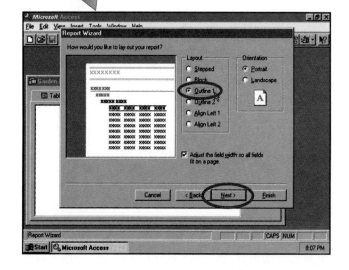

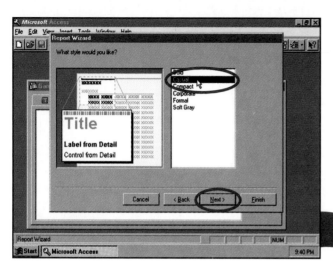

7 In this dialog box, choose a style and font for the report titles. You have six choices; click through the choices again to see what each looks like. Choose the **Casual** option from the list. Click the **Next>** button.

8 Type **Plants Listed by Color** in the text box as the title for this report. If necessary, select the **Preview the report** option button. Click the **Finish** button to complete your report.

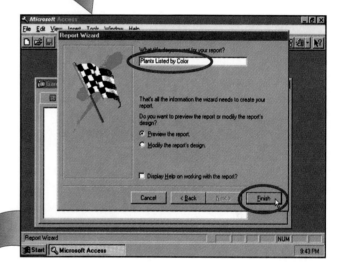

9 Increase the Report Preview window by clicking the **Maximize** button so that you can see more of the report. Notice that the mouse pointer changes shape to a magnifying glass with a minus sign in the lens. This indicates that you can shrink the display so that you can view more of the report.

10 Click anywhere on the report where the pointer appears as the magnifying glass. You see the lens changes to a plus sign. This view helps you to see the report page layout. You can quickly see if the report is centered, or too far to the left or right—but you can't read much of the text.

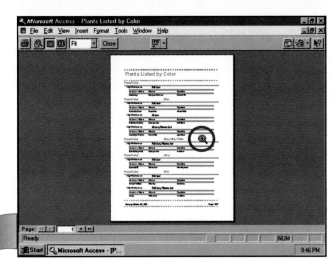

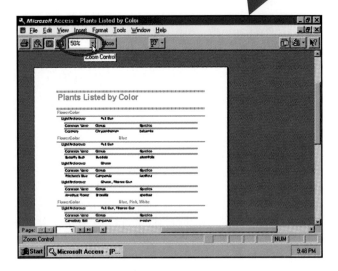

11 You can adjust the size of the report display with the Zoom Control button on the toolbar. Click the arrow on the Zoom Control button and select **50%** from the drop-down list. You see the report increase in size on your screen. Close the report by clicking the **Close** button at the corner of the window. ■

Designing a Report in Design View

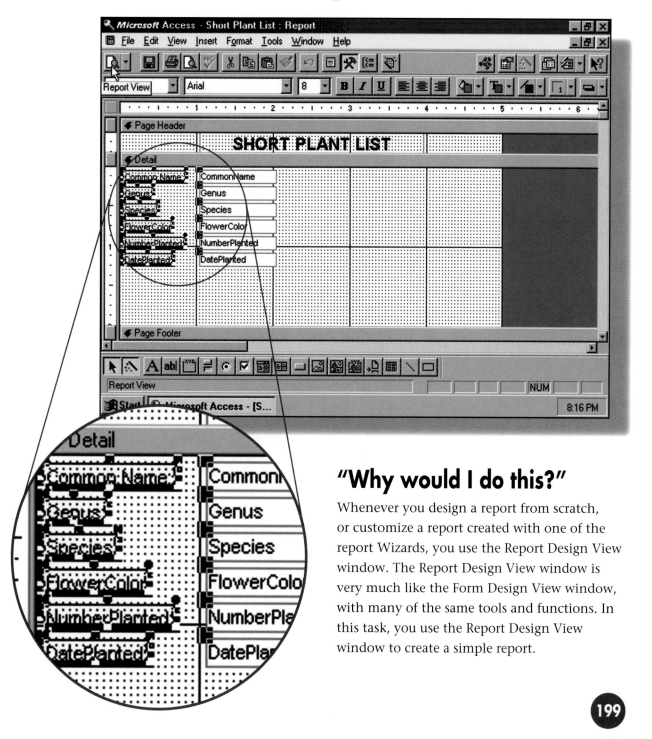

"Why would I do this?"

Whenever you design a report from scratch, or customize a report created with one of the report Wizards, you use the Report Design View window. The Report Design View window is very much like the Form Design View window, with many of the same tools and functions. In this task, you use the Report Design View window to create a simple report.

1 Click the **Reports** tab on the Database window and click the **New** button. Select **Design View** from the list on the New Report dialog box, choose the **Plants** table from the combo box, and click the **OK** button.

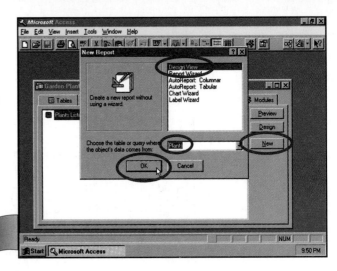

2 The report's Design View window appears. Maximize this window, if necessary, by clicking the **Maximize** button and open the field list by clicking the **Field List** button on the top toolbar.

3 Select the field **CommonName**. Now drag the field from the Field List and drop it on the report detail area.

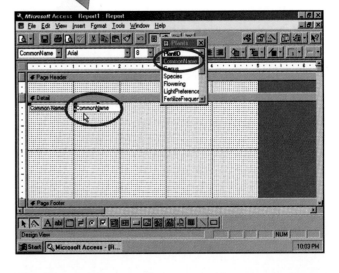

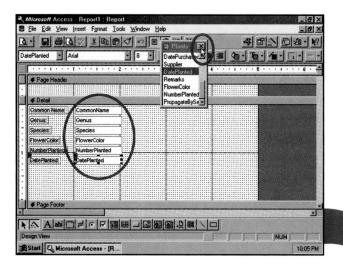

4 Now drag and drop the fields **Genus**, **Species, FlowerColor, NumberPlanted**, and **DatePlanted** onto the detail area of the report. Close the Field List dialog box by clicking its **Close** button.

NOTE

To change any of the text attributes within a label box, you must first select the label box. Access then applies any changes to all of the text within the box.

5 Click the **Label** button on the toolbox at the bottom of your screen. Move the label pointer up to the page header area of your report and click once. You see a very narrow text box with the insertion point blinking inside of it. Type **SHORT PLANT LIST** and press the **Enter** key to select the label box. Access automatically increases the size of the box to fit your label as you type.

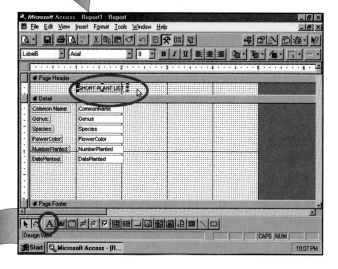

6 Click the arrow on the Font Size button in the second toolbar and choose **16** as the new font size. Next, click the **Bold** button and the **Center** button. Increase the size of the label box by dragging the lower-right handle to the bottom of the page header area and then one gridline short of the 4-inch grid line.

7 Select all of the attached label boxes in the report detail area. Click the arrow on the Special Effect button and choose the **Shadowed** button. This makes the labels stand out from the field values, making the report easier to read.

> **NOTE** ▼
>
> You can select report objects just as you select as form objects. You can use the mouse pointer to drag a box to touch each object you want to select. You can also press and hold the Shift key as you click each object you want with the mouse pointer.

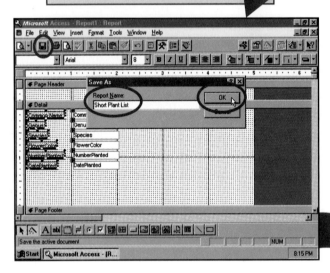

8 Click the **Save** button on the first toolbar and type **Short Plant List** in the text box in the Save As dialog box. This is the name for this report. Click the **OK** button to save the report design.

9 Click the **Report View** button to see how your report looks.

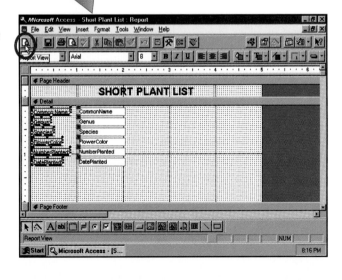

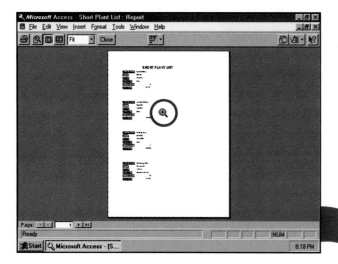

10 Click the report to view an entire page on the screen. Notice how the fields in this report are all clustered at the left margin. This needs to be corrected.

11 Click the **Close** button on the toolbar to return to the Report Design View window so that you continue to work on the report's design. ■

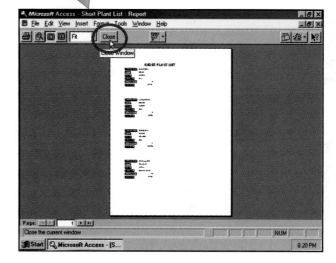

Creating Groups and Sorting

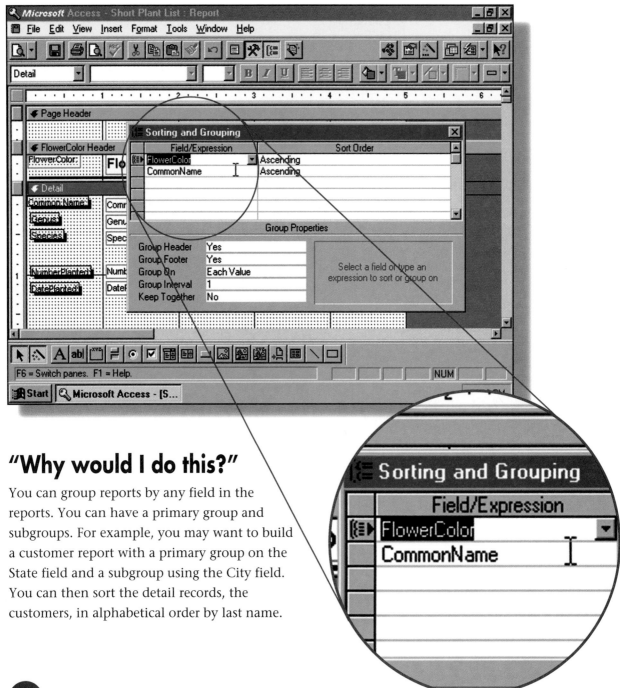

"Why would I do this?"

You can group reports by any field in the
reports. You can have a primary group and
subgroups. For example, you may want to build
a customer report with a primary group on the
State field and a subgroup using the City field.
You can then sort the detail records, the
customers, in alphabetical order by last name.

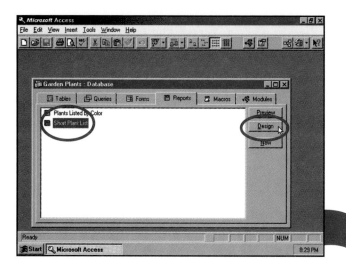

1 If not already open, select the **Short Plant List** from the Reports list in the Database window and click the **Design** button. This opens the selected report in the Report Design View window. Be sure to maximize the Design window.

NOTE ▼

You use this report as a starting point, and later you will save it under a new name.

2 Click the **Sorting and Grouping** button on the top toolbar. In the Sorting and Grouping dialog box that appears, click the arrow button and choose the **FlowerColor** field from the drop-down list.

NOTE ▼

To simply sort your report by flower color, leave the Group Header and Group Footer options on No. Access then uses the selected fields to sort your report. You can still place the sort by field within the report's detail area.

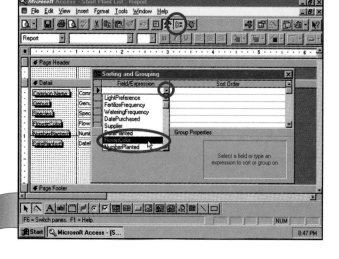

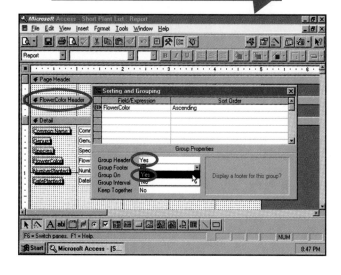

3 Select the **Yes** option in both the Group Header and Group Footer text boxes and click the **Close** button. You see Access add a FlowerColor header and FlowerColor footer to the Design View window.

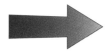

4 Close the Sorting and Grouping dialog box by clicking its **Close** button on the toolbar. Select the field **FlowerColor** from the report's detail area and drag it into the FlowerColor header area.

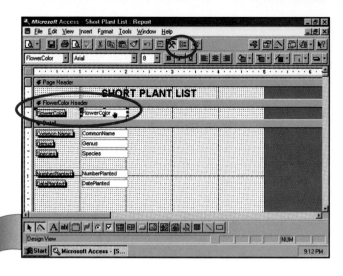

5 Increase the size of the FlowerColor field object by dragging the lower-right handle to the bottom of the header area and right to the 21/2-inch mark on the horizontal ruler. Now use the **Font Size** tool to increase the font size to **12** and click the **Bold** button.

6 Select the **FlowerColor** label and use the **Special Effects** tool (it's the one on the far right) to choose the **Flat** option. Next select the **Border Color** tool and click the **Transparent** button on the palette.

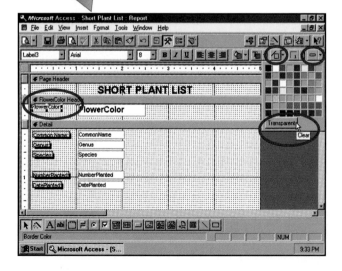

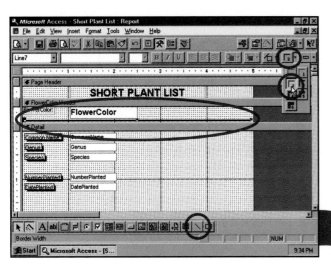

7 Click the **Line** tool on the toolbox and draw a horizontal line across the report at the bottom of the FlowerColor header area. Use the **Border Width** button and choose **2-pt Border Width** from the palette.

8 Click the **Sorting And Grouping** button to open the dialog box. Press the down arrow key once to move to the blank row and click the arrow button. Select **CommonName** from the list. All other options remain at the default settings.

> **NOTE** ▼
>
> Using the Sorting And Grouping dialog box without choosing Group Header and Footers enables you to sort detail records in either an ascending or descending order.

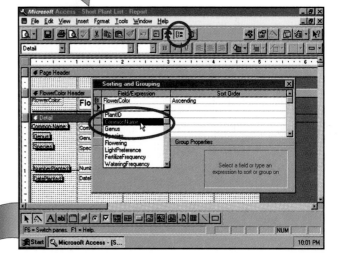

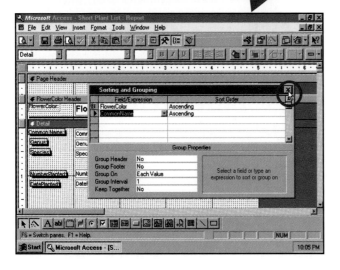

9 Click the **Close** button on the Sorting And Grouping dialog box. ■

TASK 56
Using Labels in a Report

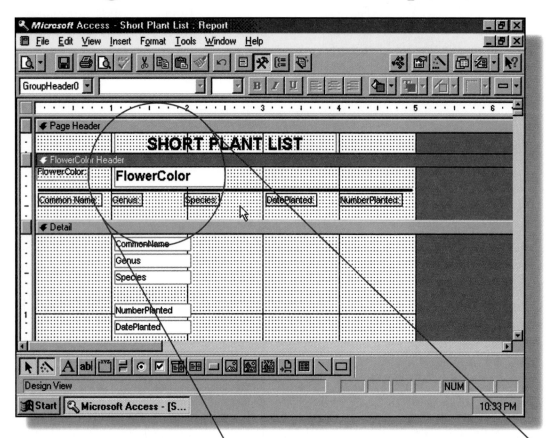

"Why would I do this?"

When building a report, you must place labels for the information contained in the report very carefully. You do not want someone who is reading the report to misinterpret what they are reading because of misaligned labels. At the same time, you do not want field labels to print for every record in the report. Printing labels once per page or per group is often enough.

208

1 Select each of the field labels in the report's detail area and move them one-by-one so that they are all in a horizontal line, in this order: Common Name, Genus, Species, Date Planted, Number Planted.

2 Select all five of the field labels and then select **Edit**, **Cut** from the menu. This removes the labels from the Design window and places them on the Windows Clipboard.

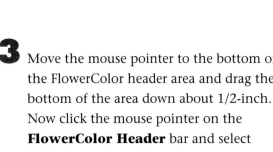

NOTE ▼

Remember, you can use the keyboard combinations Ctrl+X to cut a selected object from the window and Ctrl+V to paste the contents of the Windows Clipboard into the window.

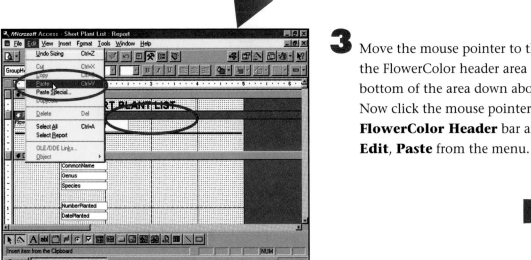

3 Move the mouse pointer to the bottom of the FlowerColor header area and drag the bottom of the area down about 1/2-inch. Now click the mouse pointer on the **FlowerColor Header** bar and select **Edit**, **Paste** from the menu.

4 The newly pasted field labels are still selected. Drag them down until they are one gridline below the line drawn across the FlowerColor header area.

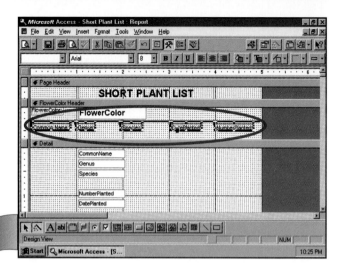

5 Click the **Properties** button, displaying the properties sheet for the selected labels. Click the **Format** tab to view these specific properties.

NOTE ▼

Remember, you can also access the property sheet for any object by double-clicking the object, or clicking the right mouse button and selecting Properties from the shortcut menu.

6 Select the **Special Effect** text box and click its arrow button. Choose the **Flat** option. Move down to the **Border Width** text box, click its arrow button, and choose **Hairline** from the list.

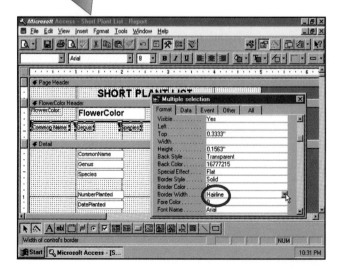

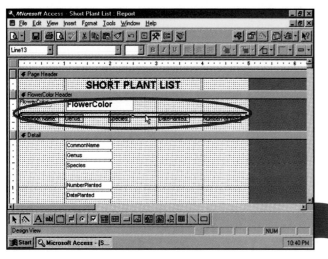

7 Close the property sheet. Select the line drawn above the labels. Press **Ctrl+C** to copy the line and then press **Ctrl+V** to paste the copy in the window.

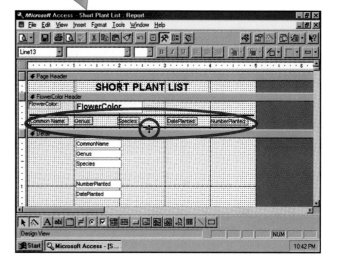

8 The copied line is automatically selected. Drag it below the labels. Now drag the bottom of the FlowerColor header area up against the new line. ■

Printing a Report

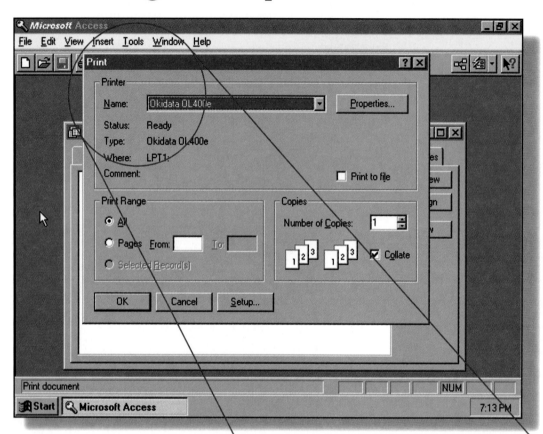

"Why would I do this?"

Once you design, refine, and view a report that you created, you are ready to show it to a larger audience. You can print a report from either the Database window or the Report Preview window.

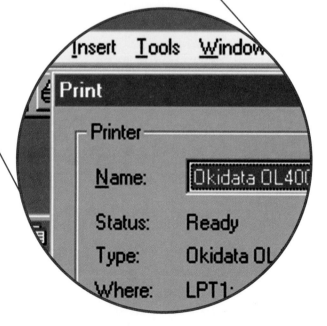

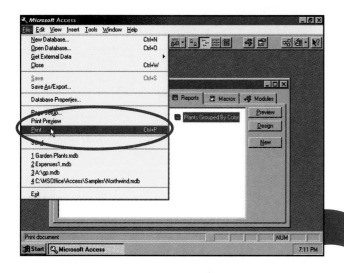

1 Open the Reports list by clicking the **Reports** tab. Select the report you want to print, **Plants Listed by Color**. Open the **File** menu and select **Print**.

NOTE ▼

You can also print a report by clicking the Print button located on both the main toolbar and the Report Preview window's toolbar.

2 You now see the Print dialog box. You can select a printer, how much or how little of the report to print, and how many copies to print. Click the **OK** button.

NOTE ▼

The printer listed in the Name text box varies depending on the printers that you have installed with Windows 95.

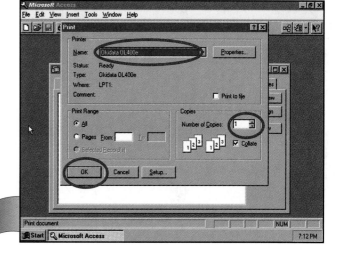

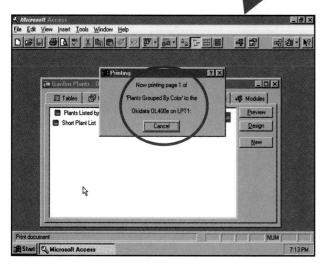

3 The Printing dialog box tells which page is currently printing, which report is being printed, and which printer is doing the work. ■

WHY WORRY?

If your printer jams, you can use the Print dialog box to print just that part of your report that didn't print. Just specify the pages you want to print.

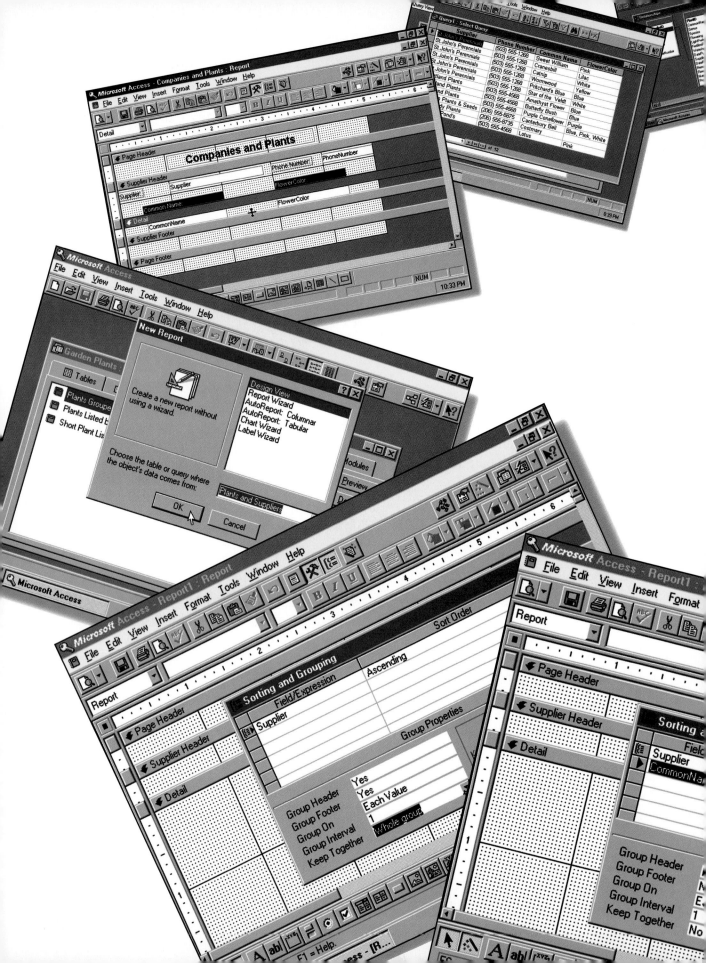

PART VII

Combining Information

The ability to combine information from multiple tables is one of the most powerful functions of a *relational database* such as Access. You usually create relationships between tables through the use of key fields. You created a key field in the Plant Suppliers table with the SupplierID field, and in the Plants table with the PlantID field. You designated both of these fields as key fields when you built the tables. By placing a copy of one table's key field in the other table, you create a relationship. For example, if you include an additional field, called SupplierID, in the Plants table, whenever you add a new plant to this table, you also include the SupplierID number for the supplier from whom you purchased the plant.

You may want to combine information from different tables for a variety of reasons:

■ To create an invoice with both customer and sales information.

■ To build a purchase order that includes supplier and product data.

■ To view quarterly sales by product.

■ To view employee sales by store.

■ To view product sales by employee.

The most common Access method for combining information is with a query. You can use a query as a funnel to pull information from two or more sources and then display the data in a form or report. Of course, this process works equally well in reverse. You can use a form that is based on a query to update and add records to each of the tables that make up the query. For example, you can create a form that displays information about a supplier, and a form that enables you to add a new supplier and a new plant—all from a single form on your screen. You can apply the same techniques to a customer and their purchases, or a supplier and your inventory.

In order for Access to use a relation between tables or queries, you must define that relationship. You create permanent relationships in the Access Relationships window. You can also create a temporary relationship between two tables when you are building a query. Any relationship you create in the Query Design window is only for that query, and for any objects such as forms or reports that are based on it.

There are several types of relationships that you can create:

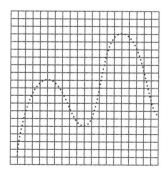

- *One-to-many* relationships are the most common type of relationship. This type of relationship exists between two tables where one table has only a single record that is linked to many records in the other table. The relationship between a customer table and an orders table is an example of this relationship. For each customer record there can be many orders.

- *One-to-one* relationships require that for each record in one table there is a single corresponding record in the second table. This relationship is not commonly seen in a relational database. If you have tables that have this relationship, you may want to consider combining them as a single table. On the other hand, you may want to divide a table with a great number of fields into two or more tables that have a one-to-one relationship, or into a table that contains sensitive information you want to keep in a separate table.

- *Many-to-many* relationships mean that for any one record of one table there are many corresponding records in the second table, while at the same time any one record of the second table also has many matching records in the first table. *You should avoid this type of relationship as it can give you unpredictable results.*

The many-to-many table can pose a quandary of sorts because it is very easy to create this type of relationship. The most obvious relationship between a table that contains information about orders and an inventory table is a many-to-many relationship—for each order you can have many products, while for each product you can have many orders. The best way out of this dilemma is to build a *bridge* table. The bridge table's entire purpose is to break the many-to-many relationship into two one-to-many relationships. A bridge table is a table that uses a *composite primary key*. A composite primary key is used when no one field by itself is unique. When building a bridge table, you usually create a composite primary key by using the primary key fields from each of the tables you want to bridge. In the sample database provided with Access, Northwind Traders (Nwind), the table "Order Details" is an excellent example of a bridge table.

As you begin to build a more complicated database, consider drawing a diagram on paper. You can include each of the tables that you have already built, and then add the tables you want to create. Place the fields for each table on the diagram and then draw lines between related tables, from one linking field to its matching field in the other table. This can help you to spot potential design problems early on.

Building a Permanent Relationship between Tables

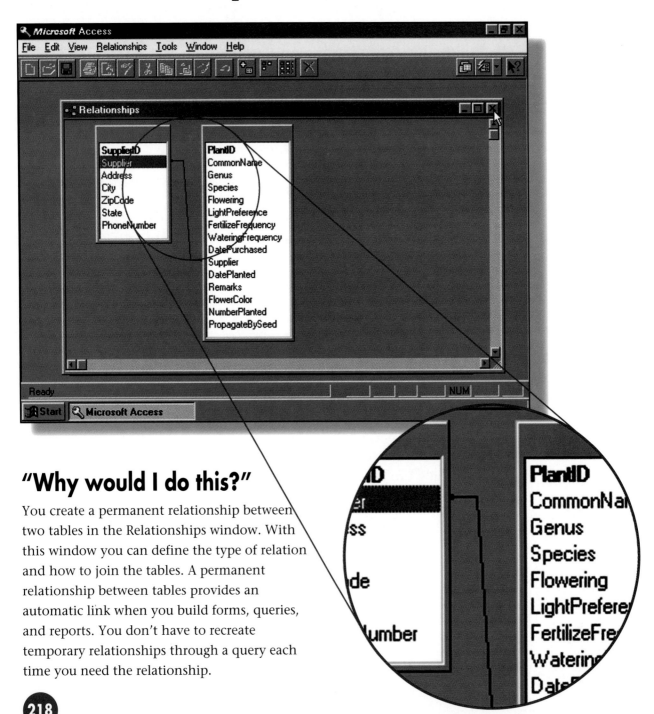

"Why would I do this?"

You create a permanent relationship between two tables in the Relationships window. With this window you can define the type of relation and how to join the tables. A permanent relationship between tables provides an automatic link when you build forms, queries, and reports. You don't have to recreate temporary relationships through a query each time you need the relationship.

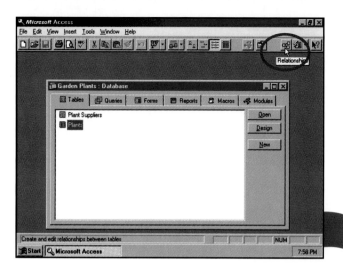

1 Open the Garden Plants database and click on the **Relationships** button on the toolbar.

WHY WORRY?

If you link the wrong fields together, simply click the Cancel button in the next dialog box, or select the line between the linked fields and press the Delete key.

2 The Show Table dialog box appears. Select the **Plant Suppliers** table and click on the **Add** button. You see the table field list appear in the Relationships window. Now select and add the **Plants** table to the Relationships window, and then click the **Close** button to remove the Show Table dialog box.

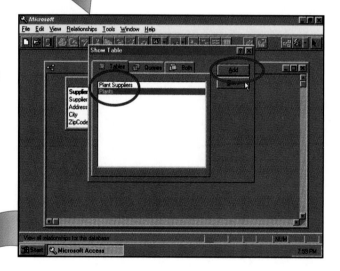

3 Increase the size of the Plants field list by dragging the bottom edge. Move the mouse pointer to the Plant Suppliers field list and click on the **Supplier** field. Drag this field to the Plants field list and drop it onto the **Supplier** field name.

4 The Relationships dialog box appears. Click the **Create** button; Access creates a permanent relationship between these tables.

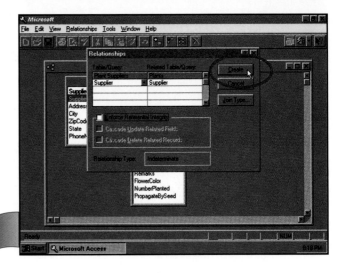

> **NOTE** ▼
>
> The field that you first select appears on the left side of the field list, and the field name that you drop the selected field on appears on the right side. If a different field name appears on either side, use the arrow button and select the correct field from the drop-down list.

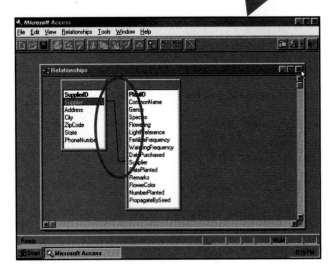

5 If Access runs into any problems when trying to create the relationship a dialog box appears. Close the Relationships window, being sure to save the layout. ■

> **WHY WORRY?**
>
> You can add additional tables to the Relationships window at any time. As you add more tables, you may want to revise the Relationships window. You can create relationships between many tables.

Using a Query with Two Tables

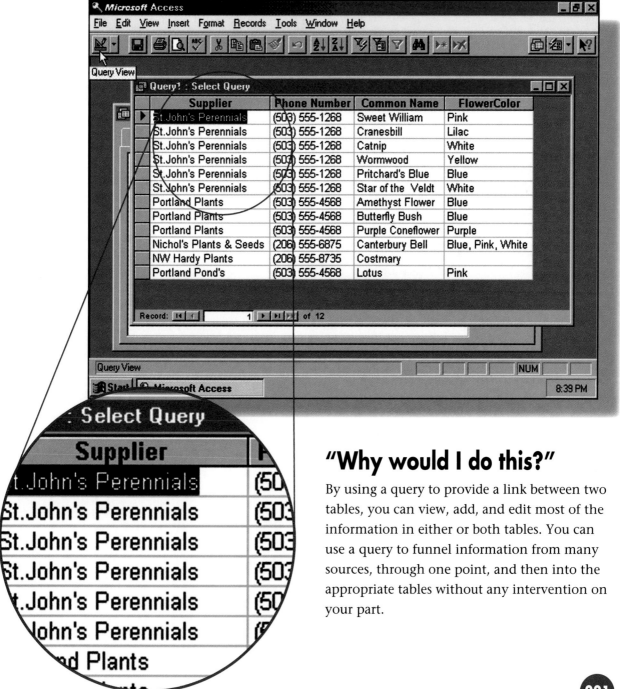

"Why would I do this?"

By using a query to provide a link between two tables, you can view, add, and edit most of the information in either or both tables. You can use a query to funnel information from many sources, through one point, and then into the appropriate tables without any intervention on your part.

1 Open the Queries list on the Database window and click the **New** button. Select **New Query** and click the **OK** button. Select the **Plant Suppliers** and **Plants** tables from the list, click the **Add** button, and then the **Close** button.

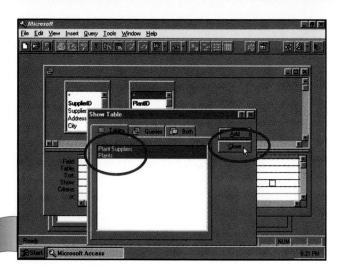

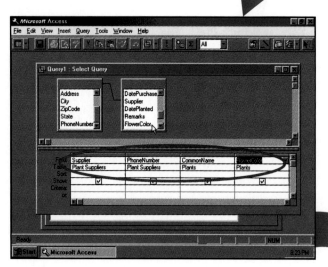

2 From the Plant Suppliers list, add the fields **Supplier** and **PhoneNumber**. From the Plants list, add the fields **CommonName** and **FlowerColor** to the query grid. Remember, you can double-click a field name to add it to the query grid.

NOTE ▼

If this query finds no records, be sure that you add records to the Suppliers table. The supplier name in the Suppliers table must exactly match the supplier name in the Suppliers field in the Plants table.

3 Click on the **Query View** button to the resulting datasheet for this query. You now see a single datasheet that lists all of your plants, the plant color, the supplier from whom you purchased the plant, and the supplier's phone number. Close and save the query with the name **Plants and Suppliers**. ■

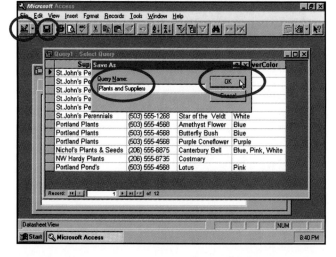

Creating a Report with a Query

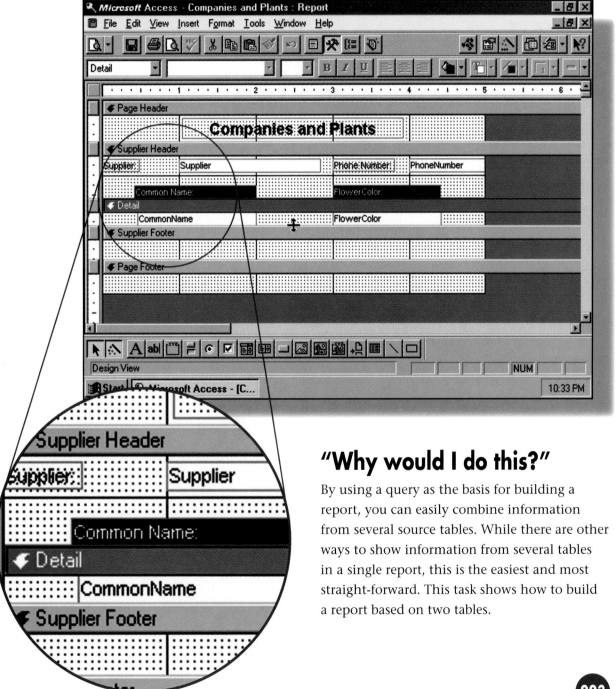

"Why would I do this?"

By using a query as the basis for building a report, you can easily combine information from several source tables. While there are other ways to show information from several tables in a single report, this is the easiest and most straight-forward. This task shows how to build a report based on two tables.

1 Select the **Reports** tab and then click the **New** button. Select **Design View** and the **Plant and Suppliers** query as the basis for the report. Be sure to maximize the window to give yourself some extra working area.

> **NOTE** ▼
>
> The Whole Group selection for the Keep Together property forces Access to break the report into pages between groups, not between detail records.

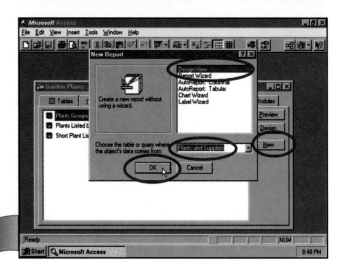

2 Click on the **Sorting and Grouping** button to display the Sorting and Grouping dialog box. Choose the **Supplier** field by selecting it from the drop-down list; this field will be used to group the report. Select **Yes** in both the Group Header and Group Footer text boxes below. Select **Whole Group** in the Keep Together text box.

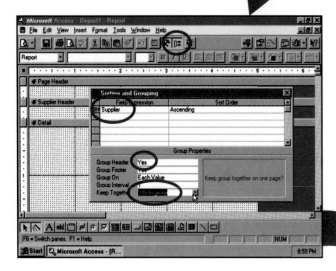

3 Move the cursor down to the next row in the Sorting and Grouping dialog box and select the field **CommonName**. The Sort Order cell displays Ascending as the sort order. Now Access sorts your detail records in an ascending order within each group. Close the dialog box.

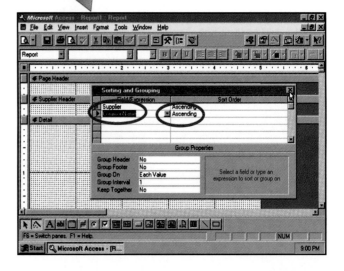

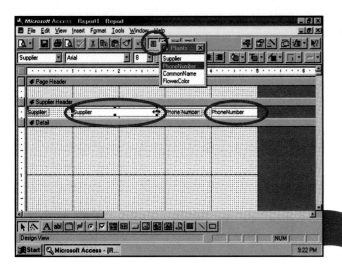

4 Open the **Field List** and place the fields **Supplier** and **PhoneNumber** in the Supplier header area of the report. Increase the length of the **Suppliers** field by selecting it and dragging it with the middle right side handle.

5 Click on the **Field List** button and place the **CommonName** and **FlowerColor** fields into the Detail area of the report. Close the field list and then move the attached labels above the fields.

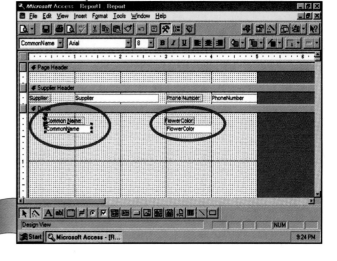

NOTE ▼

When creating a report that has a City, State, ZipCode address block consider using a text box with an expression. You can combine all three of these fields into a single text box with the expression =[City]&", "[State]&" "&[ZipCode]. You can also combine First Name, Last Name fields with a similar expression.

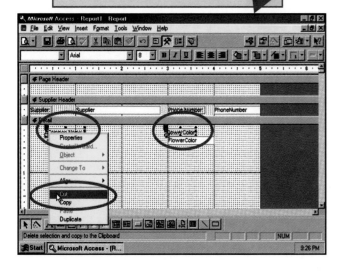

6 Select both of the attached labels in the Detail area and click the right mouse button to display a shortcut menu. Select the **Cut** option from the menu to move the labels from the report and insert them on the Windows Clipboard.

7 Move the mouse pointer to the CompanyName header bar and click on it once. Click on the right mouse button again to display the shortcut menu and select the **Paste** option. You see the labels appear at the top of the header area.

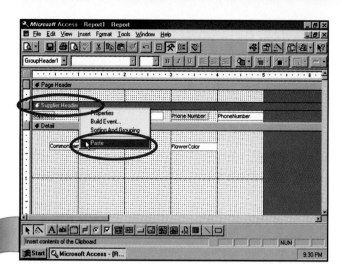

8 As a group, drag the labels down to the lower edge of the header area and place them above their fields. Drag the labels onto the Detail bar; when you let go of the mouse button, Access pushes the bar down and increases the size of the header area.

NOTE ▼

Putting the detail record labels in the group header gives you one row of labels per group; otherwise you have a label above each individual row of records, and you end up taking two lines on the report for each record instead of the one you need.

9 Increase the width of the detail record labels by dragging the right edge of one; both increase in size because they are both selected. Change the **Back Color** to black and the **Fore Color** to white to reverse the colors for the labels and set them off from the rest of the report.

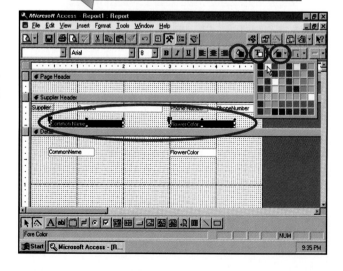

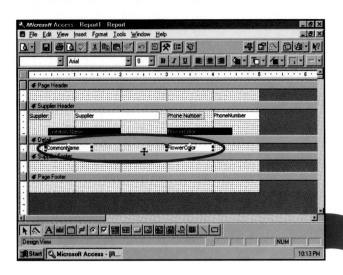

10 Select and drag both field objects in the Detail area up to the bottom of the Detail bar and then drag the Supplier footer bar up against the bottom of the fields. Increase the size of both fields to match their labels.

11 Select the **Label** tool and place a label in the Page Header area. Type **Companies and Plants** and click **Bold**, **Center**, and increase the font size to **14**. This header prints as the header for each page of your report.

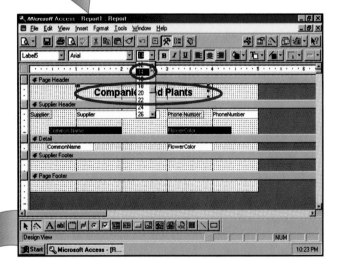

12 Select the **Line** tool and draw two lines, one above and one below the Supplier and PhoneNumber fields in the Supplier header area. Click on the **Border Width** button and select the **1-pt.** width.

13 Click the **Report View** button. Be sure to check the sort order of your groups, detail records, the totals for groups, and page layout. Make any corrections that are necessary.

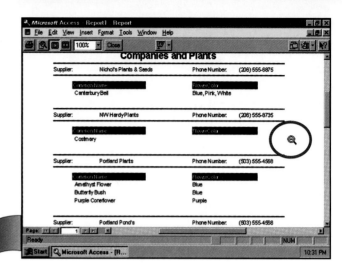

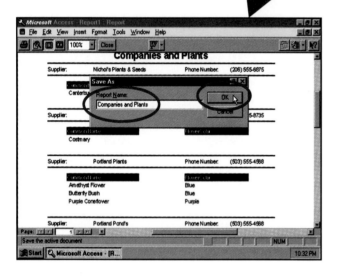

14 Open the **File** menu and select **Save**. Type **Companies and Plants** in the Save As text box and click the **OK** button to save your new report. Since this report is based on a query, each time you select the report, the query runs and provides the report with completely updated information from your tables. ■

NOTE ▼

Remember, you can also save the report by pressing Ctrl+S or the Save button on the Design View toolbar.

PART VIII

Reference

▼ Quick Reference

▼ Toolbar Guide

This final part of *Easy Access for Windows 95* includes two sections:

- A Quick Reference to Access commands and keyboard shortcuts.

- A Toolbar Guide that shows Access's main toolbars and the purpose of each tool.

Quick Reference

This Quick Reference lists the most common commands and shows you how to access the commands using the menu lists and keyboard shortcuts. Many menu lists and shortcut keys are only available in certain modes (for example, Datasheet View or Form Design View).

Menu Commands and Shortcut Keys

Feature	Command	Shortcut Key
New Database	File, New Database	Ctrl+N
Open Database	File, Open Database	Ctrl+O
Close	File, Close	Ctrl+W
Save	File, Save	Ctrl+S
Print	File, Print	Ctrl+P
Undo	Edit, Undo	Ctrl+Z
Cut	Edit, Cut	Ctrl+X
Copy	Edit, Copy	Ctrl+C
Paste	Edit, Paste	Ctrl+V
Delete	Edit, Delete	Del
Spell Checking	Tools, Spelling	F7
Insert Current Date	(none)	Ctrl+; (semicolon)
Insert Current Time	(none)	Ctrl+: (colon)
Insert Default Value	(none)	Ctrl+Alt+Spacebar
Insert Value from Previous Record	(none)	Ctrl+ ' (apostrophe), or Ctrl+" (quote mark)
Insert New Record	(none)	Ctrl+ + (plus)
Save Current Record	(none)	Shift+Enter

Feature	Command	Shortcut Key
Select a Specific Record	(none)	F5 and type record number
Toggle between Edit and Navigation mode	(none)	F2
Open Zoom Box	(none)	Shift+F2
Open Combo Box	(none)	F4, or Alt+down arrow key
Switch between Upper/Lower panes of some Design View windows	(none)	F6
Help	(none)	F1
Help with Question Mark Pointer	(none)	Shift+F1
Find	Edit, Find	Ctrl+F
Replace	Edit, Replace	Ctrl+H
Select All Records	Edit, Select All Records	Ctrl+A
Save As	File, Save As/Export	F12, or Alt+F2
Close Active Window	(none)	Ctrl+F4
Exit Microsoft Access	File, Exit	Alt+F4
Activate Database Window	Window	F11, or Alt+F1

Toolbar Guide

The Toolbar Guide shows you the toolbars that you will primarily use. This guide displays the tool's icon, name, and purpose. Not all tools are shown. The tools appear in the default order they appear in as installed with Access. You use the tools, or buttons, by simply pointing to them and clicking. Most tool actions apply only to the currently selected object. If you need help with a tool, click the Help button first and move the mouse pointer to the object that you want help with and click it. Some tools appear on more than one toolbar; the tools appear here only with the first toolbar they appear on.

Database Toolbar

Button	Name	Purpose
	New Database	Opens a new blank database
	Open Database	Opens an existing database
	Save	Saves the current object
	Print	Prints the current object
	Print Preview	Opens the current object in the Print Preview window
	Spelling	Opens and spell checks the current object, or current selection
	Cut	Cuts the current object or selection and places it on the Windows Clipboard
	Copy	Copies the current object or selection onto the Windows Clipboard
	Paste	Pastes a copy of the Windows Clipboards contents
	Undo	Undoes any changes you made to the current field or record
	Large Icons	Changes display of database objects to large icons
	Small Icons	Changes display of database objects to small icons
	List	Displays database objects with small icons in a list format
	Details	Displays database objects with file details
	Properties	Displays the current objects property sheet
	Relationships	Opens the Relationships window
	Help	Displays help for a selected object

Table, Datasheet, Form View Toolbar

Button	Name	Purpose
	Table/Query/Form/ Report View	A toggle switch between an object's Design View window and its datasheet or preview window
	Sort Ascending	Sorts the currently selected field in an ascending order
	Sort Descending	Sorts the currently selected field in a descending order
	Filter By Selection	Filters records based on currently selected information
	Filter By Form	Displays a copy of the current object to use as a selection form
	Apply/Remove Filter	Applies or Removes the current filter
	Find	Displays the Find dialog box
	New Record	Moves to the new record row
	Delete Record	Deletes the current record
	Database Window	Opens the Database Window

Table Design Toolbar

Button	Name	Purpose
	Table View	Displays a datasheet for this table
	Primary Key	Sets the selected field as the primary key
	Indexes	Displays the Indexes dialog box
	Insert Row	Inserts a blank row above the current row
	Delete Row	Deletes the current row

Query Design Toolbar

Button	Name	Purpose
	Query Type	Enables you to select a specific type of query; select, crosstab, delete, and so on.
	Run	Runs the query. An action query performs the specified action, whereas a select query displays a datasheet
	Show Table	Displays the Show Table dialog box so that you can add another table
Σ	Totals	Adds another row to the query grid so that you can add calculated expressions to your query
All	Top Values	Enables you to select only the top values in a criteria. You can choose between a certain number of records, or percentages

Form Design Toolbar

Button	Name	Purpose
	Form View	Displays the current form in the Design View window in Form View, enabling you to preview the form's design
	Field List	Displays the Field List dialog box, which contains all of the fields for the base table/query
	Toolbox	Displays the Form/Report toolbox you use to create various controls
	AutoFormat	Use to apply your choice of predefined formats to a report or form

Index

L

Label Wizard, 193
labels
    boxes
        deleting, 134
        fitting text, 134
        formatting, 201
        selecting, 136, 201
    copying, 211
    creating, 132-134
        Label Wizard, 193
    moving, 130-131
    pasting, 211
    properties sheets, 210
    records, 226
    reports, 208-211
landscape orientation,
    printing reports, 196
linking fields, 219
List Box Wizard dialog box,
    141
list boxes, 139-142
locating database files, 41

M

many-to-many relationships,
    217
maximizing windows, 129,
    200
memory (field sizes), 50
menus
    closing, 30
    commands
        hot keys, 16
        selecting, 15-17
    escape key, 17
    lists, 231

    options (control key), 16
    Start button, opening, 11
Microsoft Access command
    Programs menu, 12
Microsoft Access dialog box,
    41
Microsoft Access Help
    command (Help menu), 22
monetary amount fields, 52
mouse speeds, 11
moving
    dialog boxes, 115
    fields, 82, 101, 130-131
        columns, 105-106
    home key, 84
    labels, 130-131
    object groups, 143-145

N

naming
    database files, 42
    fields, 46, 49-50, 64
        changing, 61-62,
            64-65
        editing, 73
navigating
    backspacing, 87, 125,
        138, 142
    dialog boxes, 115
    fields, 82, 101
    forms, 144
    handles, 130
    Help window, 22-26, 28
    home key, 84
    object groups, 143-145
New Database command
    (File menu), 41
New Form dialog box, 123
New Object button, 121

New Query dialog box, 169
New Report dialog box, 195
New Table dialog box, 44, 72
no/yes fields, 54-55
number fields, 51-53

O

objects
    cutting, 209
    dragging, 64
    groups, moving, 143-145
    pasting, 209
    property sheets, 210
    reports, selecting, 202
one-to many relationships,
    217
one-to-one relationships, 217
Open Database button, 44
Open dialog box, 44
opening
    database files, 13-14, 44
    forms, 153-154
    records, 156
    Start button menu, 11
    tables, 59, 61
operators
    AND operators, 185, 187
    arithmetic operators,
        186-188
    OR operators,
        180-182, 184-185
Option buttons, 149
orders, changing
    columns, 65
    fields, 159-162
orientations (landscape), 196
OR operators, 180-182,
    184-185

P

Paste command (Edit menu), 209

pasting
 labels, 211
 objects, 209
 tables, 70

placeholders, *see* wildcards

placing, deleting fields, 156

predefined
 fields, selecting, 46
 tables, 45

primary key, 39, 74

Print command (File menu), 213

Print dialog box, 213

printing
 printers, 213
 reports, 212-213
  landscape
   orientation, 196

programs
 Access, exiting, 29
 Start button, 11

Program menu commands (Microsoft Access), 12

properties
 sheets
  labels, 210
  objects, 210
 tables, saving, 56-57

Q

QBE (Query By Example), 166

queries
 action, 167
 building, 168-170, 172

criteria
 arithmetic
  operators,
   186-188
 c*, 179
 multiple, 183
 OR operators,
  180-182, 184-185

crosstab, 167, 173-176

defined, 166

design view window, 172

fields, 170

grids, 171

inserting, 174

names, double-clicking, 178

relationships
 many-to-many, 217
 one-to-many, 217
 one-to-one, 217
 tables, 217

reports, 192, 223-228

saving, 172

select, 167-170, 172

statements, 179

suppliers tables, 222

tables
 relationships, 216
 two-way, 221-222

troubleshooting, 185

view, 172

wildcards, 179

see also searching

Query command (Insert menu), 174

Query design toolbar buttons, 234

R

records, 38
 copying between, 83-85

defined, 8

deleting, 103-104

editing, 86-88
 undo, 89-91

fields, 38

finding criteria, 180-182, 184-185

height
 fonts, 108
 resizing, 109

labels, 226

opening, 156

queries
 action, 167
 criteria, 179
 crosstab, 167
 selecting, 167
 suppliers tables, 222

replacing data, 97-99

searching, 92-96
 AND operators, 185
 criteria,
  180-182,
  184-185
 OR operators,
  180-182,
  184-185

selecting/deselecting, 104

sorting, 79, 100-102

wildcards, 177-179

relationships
 many-to-many, 217
 one-to-many, 217
 one-to-one, 217
 tables, 216-217
  building, 218-220
 windows, 220

Relationships dialog box, 220

Rename Field button, 46

Rename Field dialog box, 46

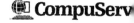
Compuserve 48px60p

Complete and Return this Card
for a *FREE* Computer Book Catalog

Thank you for purchasing this book! You have purchased a superior computer book written expressly for your needs. To continue to provide the kind of up-to-date, pertinent coverage you've come to expect from us, we need to hear from you. Please take a minute to complete and return this self-addressed, postage-paid form. In return, we'll send you a free catalog of all our computer books on topics ranging from word processing to programming and the internet.

Mr. ☐   Mrs. ☐   Ms. ☐   Dr. ☐

Name (first) ☐☐☐☐☐☐☐☐☐☐☐   (M.I.) ☐   (last) ☐☐☐☐☐☐☐☐☐☐☐☐☐☐☐

Address ☐☐☐☐☐☐☐☐☐☐☐☐☐☐☐☐☐☐☐☐☐☐☐☐☐☐☐☐☐☐

☐☐☐☐☐☐☐☐☐☐☐☐☐☐☐☐☐☐☐☐☐☐☐☐☐☐☐☐☐☐

City ☐☐☐☐☐☐☐☐☐☐☐☐☐☐☐   State ☐☐   Zip ☐☐☐☐☐ ☐☐☐☐

Phone ☐☐☐ ☐☐☐ ☐☐☐☐   Fax ☐☐☐ ☐☐☐ ☐☐☐☐

Company Name ☐☐☐☐☐☐☐☐☐☐☐☐☐☐☐☐☐☐☐☐☐☐☐☐☐☐☐☐☐

E-mail address ☐☐☐☐☐☐☐☐☐☐☐☐☐☐☐☐☐☐☐☐☐☐☐☐☐☐☐☐☐

1. Please check at least (3) influencing factors for purchasing this book.

Front or back cover information on book .... ☐
Special approach to the content .... ☐
Completeness of content .... ☐
Author's reputation .... ☐
Publisher's reputation .... ☐
Book cover design or layout .... ☐
Index or table of contents of book .... ☐
Price of book .... ☐
Special effects, graphics, illustrations .... ☐
Other (Please specify): _____ ☐

2. How did you first learn about this book?

Saw in Macmillan Computer Publishing catalog .... ☐
Recommended by store personnel .... ☐
Saw the book on bookshelf at store .... ☐
Recommended by a friend .... ☐
Received advertisement in the mail .... ☐
Saw an advertisement in: _____ ☐
Read book review in: _____ ☐
Other (Please specify): _____ ☐

3. How many computer books have you purchased in the last six months?

This book only .... ☐   3 to 5 books..................... ☐
2 books .... ☐   More than 5 .... ☐

4. Where did you purchase this book?

Bookstore .... ☐
Computer Store .... ☐
Consumer Electronics Store .... ☐
Department Store .... ☐
Office Club .... ☐
Warehouse Club .... ☐
Mail Order .... ☐
Direct from Publisher .... ☐
Internet site .... ☐
Other (Please specify): _____ ☐

5. How long have you been using a computer?

☐ Less than 6 months   ☐ 6 months to a year
☐ 1 to 3 years   ☐ More than 3 years

6. What is your level of experience with personal computers and with the subject of this book?

	With PCs	With subject of book
New	☐	☐
Casual	☐	☐
Accomplished	☐	☐
Expert	☐	☐

Source Code ISBN: 0-29236-0607-5

7. Which of the following best describes your job title?

Administrative Assistant .... ☐
Coordinator .... ☐
Manager/Supervisor .... ☐
Director .... ☐
Vice President .... ☐
President/CEO/COO .... ☐
Lawyer/Doctor/Medical Professional .... ☐
Teacher/Educator/Trainer .... ☐
Engineer/Technician .... ☐
Consultant .... ☐
Not employed/Student/Retired .... ☐
Other (Please specify): _____ ☐

8. Which of the following best describes the area of the company your job title falls under?

Accounting .... ☐
Engineering .... ☐
Manufacturing .... ☐
Operations .... ☐
Marketing .... ☐
Sales .... ☐
Other (Please specify): _____ ☐

Comments: _____
_____
_____

9. What is your age?

Under 20 ....
21-29 ....
30-39 ....
40-49 ....
50-59 ....
60-over ....

10. Are you:

Male ....
Female ....

11. Which computer publications do you read regularly? (Please list)

_____
_____
_____
_____
_____
_____
_____
_____
_____
_____

Fold here and scotch-tape